HARMONIC LEARNING

WITHDRAWN

HARMONIC LEARNING

Keynoting School Reform

James Moffett

Boynton/Cook
HEINEMANN
Portsmouth, NH

Boynton/Cook Publishers
A Subsidiary of
Heinemann Educational Books, Inc.
361 Hanover Street
Portsmouth, NH 03801
Offices and agents throughout the world

Library of Congress Cataloging-in-Publication Data
Moffett, James
Harmonic learning : keynoting school reform / James Moffett.
p. cm.
Includes bibliographical references (p.).
ISBN 0–86709-312–9
1. Learning–Social aspects. 2. Education–Social aspects–United States. 3. Interdisciplinary approach in education–United States. 4. Textbooks–Censorship–United States. 5. Educational change–United States. I. Title.
LB1060.M64 1992
370.15'23-dc20

Cover design by Twyla Bogaard
Printed in the United States of America
92 93 94 95 96 10 9 8 7 6 5 4 3 2 1

Contents

Foreword

Everything teaches. Or may teach. Every field is a potential learning field. But the fields of family, school, culture, and nature intersect and overlay each other in complicated ways that both spur and bar knowing. Any reform of public education must take fully into account how these fields do interplay now and how they might do so differently in the future.

Part 1 of this book, "Not Wanting to Know," uses a case history of school censorship as a lens to examine societal and cultural fields as they relate to the field of schooling.

Part 2, "Wanting to Know," critiques formal investigation as a way to discuss cross-cultural fields of learning and to overlay these with psychic and cosmic fields.

Against the background of these broader contexts, Part 3, "Arranging to Know," considers the subject fields of disciplines as they do and may relate to the total field of education.

In so shifting among smaller and larger fields of learning, the book switches among past, present, and future. I have attempted by these oscillations to illuminate current problems of public education and to envision some ways in which it should evolve as the movement to reform it matures.

So far, this movement has not situated education within contexts broad enough to permit thinking about it most profoundly and creatively. This results in proposals that are overly conventional and circumscribed. Most educators today advocate a more holistic approach, but how far this goes depends on how encompassing are the wholes one has in mind.

What I have tried to do here is go the whole holistic way in the sense of situating learning within "wholes" that include not only the totality of subject fields and of American society today but also "Western" culture and the pluralism of cultures past and present. This search across time and space for the biggest whole culminates in cosmology, which takes us back inward, as matter leads ultimately back to mind, to fields of consciousness that are coextensive with the fields of culture and cosmos.

The truest way to treat this ultimate holistic learning, it seems to me, is harmonically, by setting up resonances across fields. Consider consciousness, culture, and cosmos as octaves of reality spanning from infra to ultra. Then thoughts about one field will reverberate within another. The frequencies of these overtones differ across fields but only as integral multiples of each other, harmonically. Thus a note struck one place will resound in another in the terms of that other, sometimes loudly nearby, sometimes faintly afield, in just the way that learning something in the physical, emotional, intellectual, or spiritual domain affects all domains at once, each according to its register.

Acknowledgments

A version of "Not Wanting to Know" appeared in *English Education,* volume 21, number 2 (May 1989) as "Censorship and Spiritual Education" and is reprinted with permission of the National Council of Teachers of English. A shorter version appeared under that title in *The Right to Literacy,* edited by Andrea Lunsford, Helene Morgan, and James Slevin, 1990, and is reprinted with the permission of the publisher, the Modern Language Association. A different short version appeared as "Varieties of Censorship" in *The Journal of Educational Thought,* volume 24, number 3A (December 1990) and is reprinted with permission.

Portions of "Wanting to Know" appeared as "Current Issues and Future Directions" in *Handbook of Research on Teaching the English Language Arts,* edited by James D. Flood, *et al.* copyright 1991 by the National Council of Teachers of English and the International Reading Association. It's reprinted with permission of Macmillan Publishing Company.

Part I

Not Wanting to Know

The authors of the Declaration of Independence of the United States and of the Constitution were rightly expecting any tyranny to come from government, because at that time it was monarchies that violated human and civil rights. Among these abuses, censorship figured prominently as a means of quelling political opposition and enforcing social conformity. Wise as were the founding fathers, they could not foresee that when government decreed personal liberty and free enterprise, it set up the possibility of tyranny in a new quarter, the private sector, against which they provided little protection. In granting the rights to individuals and corporations that we so proudly vaunt today, modern democracies in effect also relegated to special-interest groups the powers of former tyrants.

In ancient Rome a censor was an official who kept a census for taxation purposes and also censured vice. We are left to wonder what bound sin and taxes so closely together. At any rate, the justification for censoring has traditionally been moral, whether initiated by government or by special-interest groups, as today. Of course, since these groups lobby officials to legislate their will, democratic government does again become party to censorship. But it seldom instigates the suppression of works from the private sector as totalitarian regimes routinely do. (Democratic governments protect themselves through covert operations and cover-ups of their own actions.)

Whether wielded by the public or the private sector, censorship expresses the will and values of some part of society contending with other factions about what people are to know. It concerns education not just because somebody wants to ban some school books but because it shows us in a blatant way how social division chronically curtails knowledge in and out of school. Censorship is manifold. In some form, at some level, we are all censoring, because we all want to control others' behavior, and our own, by controlling knowing.

Fundamentalist Insurrection

In 1974 the most tumultuous and significant textbook controversy that North America has ever known broke out in Kanawha County, West Virginia. The textbooks teachers choose from today are limited by what happened there then. The school district of Kanawha County yokes together the sophisticated city of Charleston with forests of chemical smokestacks strung along the upper Kanawha River valley and, in the lower valley, with some of the most primitive rural society in America. Ignoring the fundamentalist Appalachian part of its constituency, the district selected $450,000 worth of reading and language arts textbooks that fulfilled a state mandate for multicultural materials. Among these figured a K–12 program that I had directed called Interaction.

One member of the five-person school board was a fundamentalist minister's wife, elected for her success in earlier quashing a sex-education program. She had challenged the proposed books the previous spring but lost when the selections came to a vote. She succeeded, however, in stirring opposition that grew over the summer as she and others passed around excerpts from the books at local meetings.

By the time school started on September 3, the book protesters had organized themselves for tough activist tactics borrowed from the labor movement. Led by fundamentalist ministers from the hills and hollows of the upper valley, they kept their children home from school and threatened parents who did not, picketed mines until the miners struck, barricaded some trucking companies, demonstrated outside the school board building in defiance of court injunctions, and on September 10 got city bus drivers to suspend service.

The next day the board announced it was withdrawing the books until a citizens review committee could report on them. But disruption escalated. At each of two picket points a man was wounded by gunfire. Cars were smashed, and a CBS television crew was roughed up. Extremist protesters fired on school buses returning from their rounds and even firebombed two elementary schools at night. Leaders of both sides were threatened and guarded. On September 13, the safety of both children and adults seemed so much at risk that the superintendent shut down all public schools for a four-day weekend, during which he and the school board slipped out of town. The whole county bordered on anarchy.

After delaying its climactic meeting for a week, following a dynamite blast in its building, the school board voted November 8 on the recommendations of its citizens review committee. The majority of the committee asked for the reinstatement of virtually all of the books, and the minority rejected virtually all the books. The board decided to reinstate all but the most controversial series and the senior high portion of Interaction, which were consigned to libraries. Protest activities abated when Governor Arch Moore finally allowed state troopers to reinforce county sheriffs, and ended in the spring, after one of the ministers leading the revolt was sentenced to three years in prison for his part in firebombing a school. By then the superintendent and head of the board had both resigned. The anathematized books became too hot to handle and so might as well not have been returned. Ill feeling remained for many years among antagonists in the schools and homes of Kanawha County. The controversy drew international attention and stirred widespread debate.

During the autumn in which this drama unrolled, outsiders from Communists to the Ku Klux Klan showed up to take sides, but most connections were made by right-wing groups seeking to annex West Virginia into the national censorship network and into conservative political movements, which were forming up the New Right. Among these outsiders were Mel and Norma Gabler, whose nonprofit corporation for reviewing textbooks has made Longwood, Texas, the textbook censorship capital of the nation. Edward Jenkinson, former chair of the Committee Against Censorship of the National Council of Teachers of English, asserted to the press that "the Gablers are the two most important people in education," and some textbook editors admit that they keep copies of the Gablers' critiques before them as they work. The Gablers joined the protest leaders in talks and rallies around Charleston, sent them objections they had written on books up for adoption in Texas, and taught them how to write their own objections for the minority report of the citizens review committee.

Censoring leads to precensoring. Teachers, librarians, and administrators often rule out in advance books that may provoke such turbulence. They internalize the censors' criteria. But the most serious precensoring goes on in editorial offices. No publisher has dared since 1974 to put out language arts or literature textbooks having the range of subject matter, points of view, and multicultural integrity as those attacked in Kanawha County. As Texas goes, so goes the nation. Not only is this conservative state the largest single adoption market but books adopted there gain the selling advantage of having been so sanitized that they're safe anywhere—the rightist equivalent of the Good Housekeeping Seal of Approval. The biasing of textbooks is actually a far greater problem in other subjects than English. Consider government, economics, history, and other social studies, which can never be impartially treated even in books not having to pass the Texas test.

Although the textbooks U.S. teachers may choose from today were determined by what happened once in Kanawha County and what happens all the time in Texas, the government of neither state is to blame. The West Virginia Department of Education had mandated open-minded multicultural adoption criteria that obviously influenced Kanawha County's liberal adoptions. And the Texas Adoption Agency hardly shares the views of the famed Gablers and other zealots who make skillful use of the democratic forum that the agency sponsors before adopting. When Texas does choose confectionary books, as it often does, it's because its constituency wants them. This too is democracy in action and is no doubt why George Orwell could at times rouse himself to only two cheers for it. In granting liberty to individuals and corporations, Western civilization did not at the same time teach people how to grant it to each other. Developing an inner breadth commensurate with the outer freedom clearly remains a job for the future.

My publisher started phasing out Interaction the next year on grounds that the program had not earned enough by its third year, according to their corporation formula; but loud censorship rows terrify textbook publishers, who fear for the company's name and will sacrifice one program to salvage their whole line of school offerings. The other publishers of major programs involved in the controversy either killed them or sanitized them by revision. The religious conversion that amoral corporations have undergone to accommodate fundamentalist censors symbolizes the ludicrous union that has occurred between the moralistic and materialistic factions in the private sector.

The Kanawha County rebellion lent great energy not only to the national censorship movement, which grew at a heady rate during the Reagan administration, but also to the rise of evangelical politics and to the New Right itself that boosted Reagan into the White House. The Heritage Foundation, a conservative Washington think tank that was so close to the Reagan administration as to have helped draft some of its legislation, sent legal aid to the protest leaders who were being jailed in Kanawha County. The old intimacy between politics and religion, glossed over in our secular age, has been thrust into the foreground since 1974 as fundamentalism has consolidated into a major political force in Christendom and Islam. What connects politics and religion today is ethnocentricity, the heart of the textbook dispute.

Inner Censorship versus Self-Knowledge

The creek preachers have done me a great favor. They have made me think about the many ways we all suppress knowledge outside and repress it inside—and about why we do. But to broach this intricate subject let's look at what these fundamentalists objected to in the books. In 1982 I interviewed three of the protest leaders in Kanawha County. I have studied carefully the criticisms that dissenting members of the citizens review committee wrote about particular selections in the disputed books. I have written an account and interpretation of the Kanawha County controversy as a book, *Storm in the Mountains: A Case Study of Censorship, Conflict and Consciousness* (1988a). In trying to see more deeply by the light of this incendiary episode, I have honored most what meant most to the objectors, their religious beliefs and values.

In plain human terms, the protesters feared losing their children. Books bypass the oral culture—hearth and ethos—and thus may weaken local authority and control. Perhaps all parents fear having their children mentally kidnapped by voices from other milieus and ideologies. The rich range of ideas and viewpoints, the multicultural smorgasbord, of the books adopted in Kanawha County were exactly what fundamentalists don't want. They believe that most of the topics English teachers think make good discussion are about matters they consider already settled. They feel that the invitation to reopen them through pluralistic readings, role playing, values clarification, personal writing, and open-ended discussion can only be taken as an effort to indoctrinate their children in the atheistic free thinking of that eastern-seaboard liberal establishment that scoffs at them and runs the country according to a religion of Secular Humanism.

The book protesters charged that our books attacked family, church, and state—authority in general. As the most exclusive social unit of all, the family is the heart of hearts of the culture. Hearth and ethos. Consanguinity and contiguity. Blood and soil. And so the pro-family movement served as nucleus for the New Right and its anti-Communist jihad. As an example of attacking the family, the reviewers cited an excerpt from *The Children of Sanchez,* one of anthropologist Oscar Lewis's studies of the culture of poverty, based mainly on the participants' own accounts. The objection begins with a very just observation: "The father Sanchez is strict, beats his boys, etc. But when they turn out wrong, he rationalizes." Then the objections:

1. The story is deliberately concocted to belittle parents and their knowledge about how to raise children.
2. This story belittles discipline.
3. Does this story place the entire blame of failure on the part of the parent? Doesn't the school have some responsibility?
4. If the editors or author understood children and "the process of education" they wouldn't need to blame the parents. They would know what to do! (pp. 171–72)*

Gina Berriault's short story "The Stone Boy" provided another example of attacking the family. A nine-year-old boy accidentally shoots and kills his older brother as, carrying rifles, they go to pick peas early one morning. His parents and the sheriff can't understand why he goes on to pick peas for an hour before telling them and why he remains so unemotional. The boy tries that night to go to his mother, but she sends him away from the door. In their summary,

* These and other objections below are quoted from an unpublished, unpaginated typescript written by dissenting members of the citizens Textbook Review Committee. The pages cited here and below are from *Storm in the Mountains* (Moffett, 1988a), where the disapproved selections are treated in more detail.

the reviewers said at this point, "The rest of the story relates his feelings about his mother, etc.," and they misquote the narration as follows: "He had come to clasp her in his arms and to pommel her breasts with his head." The rest of the story is not about his feelings for his mother but about how everyone turns against him because they think he is unnatural not to show feeling. Thus rejected, he does indeed start to harden. By not understanding, the family has lost *two* boys. The objections were:

1. The story is abnormal. It should not be used in the classroom.
2. The classroom is not a "sensitivity-training" laboratory.
3. Teachers are not trained to deal with abnormal situations. Who is dictating that this type material be used in the classroom and why?
4. Why don't the educators eliminate the problems? Why don't they do some positive research to help the student? They are failures—as well as the parents.

Now for the correct quotation: "He had come to clasp her in his arms and, in his terror, pommel her breasts with his head." Was it suppression or repression that omitted "in his terror" and left instead the innuendo of incest? By avoiding the inner life, both the parents in the story and the reviewer of the story missed what the author made very plain by many other indications than this, that this boy is not stony, he's petrified. (pp. 179–83).

Had I wanted to attack the family I would have quoted Christ from Matthew 10:34–36:

> Think not that I am come to send peace on earth; I came not to send peace but a sword.
>
> For I am come to set a man at variance against his father, and the daughter against her mother, and the daughter-in-law against her mother-in-law.
>
> And a man's foes shall be they of his own household.

Hardly sounds like a spokesperson for the pro-family movement, does it? Now, of course, Christ is speaking in the hyperbole of the spiritual master trying to wake us up from our conditioning. The sword is to cut attachments that interfere with spiritual development. This is why the Lord tested Abraham by telling him to sacrifice Isaac. Christ continues (Matthew 10:37): "He that loveth father or mother more than me is not worthy of me: and he that loveth son or daughter more than me is not worthy of me." Attachment to family is the prototype of the attachments to race, nation, and ethos that, when put first, distract the pilgrim from the way.

All of the programs denounced in Kanawha County contained works by modern poets trying to make Christ real to today's secular readers. In an Interaction book of narrative verse for high school we included two such poems, one of which was Charles Causeley's "Ballad of the Bread Man."

> Mary stood in the kitchen
> Baking a loaf of bread.
> An angel flew in through the window,
> "We've a job for you," he said.

In this light style it goes on to tell the Nativity as it might happen today, but through the breezy manner we hear a reverential note that sounds the real meaning of the poem. Christ is imagined as a "bread man."

> He went round to all the people
> A paper crown on his head.
> Here is some bread from my father.
> Take, eat, he said.
>
> Nobody seemed very hungry
> Nobody seemed to care
> Nobody saw the god in himself
> Quietly standing there.

The objectors called this "A mockery of Christ's birth and life."

T. S. Eliot's "Journey of the Magi" brought out a more significant misunderstanding. Recall the last portion:

> All this was a long time ago, I remember
> And I would do it again, but set down
> This set down
> This: were we led all that way for
> Birth or Death? There was a Birth, certainly,
> We had evidence and no doubt. I had seen birth and death
> But had thought they were different; this Birth was
> Hard and bitter agony for us, like Death, our death.
> We returned to our places, these Kingdoms,
> But no longer at ease here, in the old dispensation,
> With an alien people clutching their gods.
> I should be glad of another death.

Objection: "This poem is a take-off on the Bible. The birth they say was 'Hard and bitter agony for us like Death, our death.' It is poking fun of the birth of Jesus" (162–64).

Eliot capitalized "birth" and "death" in the abstract sense and used lowercase for the physical sense. The literalism that gives fundamentalists their name keeps them from realizing that the poem is about their favorite subject—being born again—which is indeed the central spiritual experience of any religion. But fundamentalists have an authoritarian notion of it that prevents them from recognizing it. In the passive redemption of evangelism, Jesus does all the saving. The guilty sinner has only to quit screwing up and hand his life over. The magi, on the other hand, have made a desperately difficult journey that has ended in a shattering of the old egocentric, ethnocentric life. Witnessing the new star and the radiant infant made the magi see the light of higher realms exactly as the Transfiguration of the adult Christ later did Peter, James, and John. This trauma marks the birth of the spiritual self, as rendered in shamanic myths of being dismembered and reassembled and as undergone in the three-day, out-of-body burial entrancements of the ancient Mysteries, exemplified in the story of Lazarus and symbolized in the entombment and resurrection of Christ himself.

Plato banished the poets from his republic because he thought literature would more likely fasten an audience on the forms of life than direct them to the invisible reality that the forms merely manifest. But the reader of scripture runs precisely the same risk, especially if literal-minded. And who is not too much so?

So it was that the textbooks were alleged to have attacked family and church. How about state now? A couple of Interaction books contained interviews and trial transcripts that allowed students to hear what a number of participants in the Vietnam war had to say, including some involved in the civilian massacre at My Lai. These were condemned as unpatriotic, un-American, and "pacifist," an epithet of denunciation and a synonym for "traitor." Actually, the testimony of Lt. Calley arouses considerable sympathy for an officer in a war where those you are to kill and those you are to protect all look alike. The objection to the Vietnam interviews was that they were "not necessary for education" and seemed included only to make students "feel guilt and shame."

The issue of this Vietnam material was self-examination, which the censors chronically resisted. In fact, one of the set terms used throughout the censorship network in reviewing books is "invasion of privacy," a liberal-sounding objection that is invoked whenever, for example, students are invited to relate literature to their own experience or to talk or write about their thoughts and feelings. One of the set terms used in the literature of psychological research on authoritarian or dogmatic personality is "anti-intraception"—fear of inwardness, something, incidentally, that women frequently attribute to men. Indeed, we shouldn't lay just at the door of conservative censors this preference for projecting onto others instead of looking within, for self-exoneration over self-examination. As John Barth quipped in his novel *Giles Goat Boy,* "Self-knowledge is bad news."

The injunction against "invasion of privacy" conflicts with the ancient spiritual adage "Know thyself," which is the ground of all inquiry. It does not mean merely to understand your personal quirks but your transpersonal traits as well—your individual nature, human nature, and nature all at once inasmuch as you are a microcosm of the macrocosm of the world. "Know thyself" was the supreme tenet of spiritual education well before Oedipus discovered that he was the culprit he sought. But it was never meant to be a guilt trip. That is the negative view, based on a low self-concept, the main trait, by the way, that researchers find in the authoritarian or dogmatic personality.

Molting lesser selves can be painful and feel like destruction, as Eliot's magi said. Some things we don't want to know, not just the bad news but, yes, the good news too, the awesome possibility of being far more than we think we are. Most of us don't want to believe Christ when he said, "Ye are gods." We'd rather just keep playing schlemiel. Pursuing the question "Who am I?" to whatever depth and height we can bear the answer is a cosmic voyage that should be the first goal statement in every school district's curriculum guide, before that stuff about being good citizens and productive workers. Those will happen as fallout from self-development.

Now I want to connect "invasion of privacy" with another of the most common objections in the censorship network—morbidity and negativity. "Trash, cover to cover" was the verdict of the Kanawha County reviewer of an Interaction book for senior high called *Monologue and Dialogue,* which contained Walter de la Mare's "The Tryst," Robert Browning's "Soliloquy of the Spanish Cloister," William Blake's "The Clod and the Pebble," John Keats's "Ode to a Nightingale," Matthew Arnold's "Dover Beach," Richard Wilbur's "Two Voices in the Meadow," Paul Laurence Dunbar's "Jealous," and stories by John O'Hara and J. F. Powers. What English majors were taught to regard as masterpieces, or at least chestnuts, of literature were summarized as follows in reviewing a book from another program:

> "The Highwayman," Alfred Noyes—Girl shoots herself through the breast.
>
> "Lord Randall," traditional ballad—The main character is poisoned.
>
> "Danny Deaver," Rudyard Kipling—Poem concerning a military hanging.
>
> "The Tell-Tale Heart," E. A. Poe—A man cunningly contrives to kill an old man whom he loves, carries this out and dismembers him.
>
> "To Build a Fire," Jack London–A man freezes to death. (p. 128)

On this basis we could dismiss "Ode to a Nightingale" as suicidal and "Dover Beach" as nihilistic and proceed to eliminate not only tragedy itself but virtually all literature.

And yet the case the censors make differs not a great deal from Plato's reason for banishing the poets. Dwelling on Barth's "bad news"—realism—just keeps you down. Why not keep fixed on the good news, gospel, the word of God? Indeed, another ancient spiritual dictum is "You become what you think." If you focus on the negative, you will become or remain negative. If you meditate on the divine, you will bring out your divinity. But if I'll become what I think, and if I work to know myself, isn't this a prescription for disaster, if I'm also rotten? And there's the crux of it all. The spiritual assumption is that one is not rotten to the core, innately depraved, but a god at heart who has to work down through the rottenness to the deeper self, rejoin the original essence. This is why the negative self-concept makes great literature look like only bad news—not "There but for the grace of God go I" but merely "My God, there go I." In lit crit circles this would be called lack of esthetic distance.

As religious education was phased out of public schools in the last century, English education was phased in. Literature took over from scripture, literary criticism from Biblical exegesis, textual performance from liturgical service. The syllabus is now the canon, the lit prof the hierophant. Has English teaching extended religious teaching in a secular way? If so, is that right? If not, should it?

Literary artists themselves, I wager, see their work as gospel, as good news, even though it may be wrought from the bad news of self-examination and other worldly realities, because they feel the transformative effect of the imagination. I don't just mean that they manipulate reality to make it satisfy some emotion important to them, though that happens too. I mean that the bad news or rottenness is illuminated, is placed against or shot through with some new light, or that the things of this world are so newly connected and patterned that they coalesce into a new reality. Creativity belies its own negative subject matter. Literature is a secular form of scripture and indeed is descended from it. Holy writ deals with negative things but to show the good news in the bad news. In its own secular way literature tries to do this too. If read shallowly, literally, both can be dangerous because their rhetorical power and spellbinding stories *can,* as Plato worried, attach readers even more to surfaces than they already are.

We resist looking inward in the measure we fear what we will find there, namely, the uncontrollable and unacceptable feelings we cannot tolerate in consciousness. Suppose we have grown up in an environment that has permitted no criticism of elders or other expression of negative feeling and has made us believe we fall hopelessly below some high standards we should be meeting. We feel both worthless and enraged. Then we have too much inside to bear disturbing. If you insist that you have nothing inside yourself corresponding to what these literary works are about, then you can claim that others are imposing their morbidity on you. To the extent we deny the inner life, we can't set up the correspondences necessary to understand things outside, including what's in books. It is in this way that self-knowledge is the gateway to other knowledge.

Ethnocentric Limitations

The accusation that our books attacked family, church, and state is exactly the same that Jesuits and other émigrés leveled against Freemasonry in the wake of the French Revolution. The fundamentalist protesters said that a Communist conspiracy in government and education had placed our books in their schools. It has been a running mistake throughout history to construe efforts to expand consciousness as attacks on everything we know and hold dear. The

Jesuits charged that Freemasons fomented the French Revolution to overturn world order as a continuation of a heretical conspiracy against family, church, and state reaching back across various secret societies into antiquity. These Appalachian fundamentalists were unwittingly perpetuating a conspiracy theory of some two hundred years' standing that persists today in much better educated groups such as the John Birch Society, who simply substituted Communists for Freemasons but kept the belief in a conspiracy pledged to fighting their Christianity to the death. Indeed, really scholarly ultrarightists can show you how Freemasonry naturally led into Communism and how both derived via the Knights Templar and medieval heresies from pre-Christian cults in the evil East.

But generally the Kanawha County objections broke the religious framework down into social issues familiar as planks in the platforms of the Moral Majority, Renaissance Canada, and the pro-family movement. The censors were for the Vietnam War and other anti-Communist military action, tougher treatment of criminals, corporal punishment of children, school prayer (if Christian), literal interpretation of the Bible, free enterprise, good grammar, and phonics. They stood against pacifism, socialism, the women's movement, abortion, gay rights, dirty words, sexual references, and relativity. Sharing these stands with national organizations may owe partly to their reading and hearing what these other conservatives were saying, but people of the same psychological makeup tend toward the same social and political positions anyway.

Another of the set phrases riding the censorship circuits that was often invoked against the disputed books is "situation ethics." This abhorrence of moral relativism rules out discussions of right and wrong in the behavior of literary characters or in one's own life. The basic idea of fundamentalism, after all, is literalism, that there is only one way to read either books or reality—oddly, the most material way. Some ultrarightist intellectuals are now mounting arguments against the theory of relativity. Einstein bids fair to replace Darwin as the preferred hate object, which comes close to Hitler's repudiation of "Jewish physics." "Situation ethics" expresses, I venture, a deep need to recoil from alternatives of any sort, whether alternative readings of a text, alternative viewpoints in thought, alternative courses of action, or alternative social groups.

Fundamentalists want school to reinforce the race spirit and the home culture not only by excluding alternatives but also by subverting inquiry. The censors really wanted to fill up schooling with rote learning of facts and avoid student thinking. They wanted, for example, more grammar, which has no subject matter, and less literature, which indeed has content, often entirely too thought-provoking. Like phonics, which they also advocate, grammar is in itself meaningless. A contentless curriculum would perfect censorship. Only an authoritarian approach can enforce a curriculum tending that way of course, but then authoritarianism is part and parcel of ethnocentric exclusivity.

The book protesters could not admit one of their main objections, because it was racist. They rejected virtually all of the reading selections by blacks and Hispanics, but the reasons they cited were bad grammar, vulgar language, revolutionary ideology, irrelevance of ghetto life to their children's environment, and racism against whites. Some of their objections were anti-Semitic. Actually, there are relatively few blacks, Jews, and Hispanics in West Virginia, which is a pocket culture. Their real fear is of the Other, any other. They resented references to other cultures and other religions. They inveighed against Interaction books of folk literature such as fables, legends, and parables because they were international. Extremist conservative intellectuals despise the United Nations because it transcends nationalism, on which their identity is partially founded. Such people automatically distrust any international movement, from Communism to ecumenicism. Anti-Semitism may go back in part to the Diaspora, which internationalized Jews. The very fact of being international may be taken as evidence of conspiracy and in any case threatens the ethnocentricity that censorship is mainly about.

The One and the Many

Fundamentalist censors have performed a great public service. They have forced educators to face some issues we have avoided for generations. First is the pretense that schooling need not be involved in moral and spiritual matters and indeed cannot, in the United States, legally be involved because of the First Amendment separation of church from state. But the founding fathers certainly did not intend for public education to breed materialism, as the fundamentalists rightly complain that it does.

Modern intellectuals have reason to distrust the word "spiritual," and I've certainly hesitated about using it because it's apt to trigger associations that will smother my other words. But I haven't found any better term. So I'll try to refurbish it a bit. I think I can do this best if I first distinguish spirituality from morality and religion. Morality concerns good and bad behavior. As the root meanings of both "morals" and "ethics" indicate, these come from the *customs* of some group, an ethos. Morality is caught, not taught. *Knowing* right is not so much the problem as *doing* it, and most reasons for not doing it are very extracurricular, involving, in fact, all the rest of the culture, some of which may very well contradict the morals, which at any rate hardly apply to treatment of *outsiders*.

As *its* root meaning suggests, religion aims to tie the individual back to some less apparent reality from which he or she has been diverted by, presumably, people and other attractive hazards in the environment. However divinely inspired, any religion partakes of a certain civilization, functions through human institutions, and is therefore culturally biased. Spirituality is the perception of oneness behind plurality. Spiritual *behavior* is the acting on this perception. Morality follows from spirituality, because the more that people identify with others the better they act toward them. The supreme identification, of oneself with the One, brings about that reunion toward which religions work, at the same time that it makes morality apply beyond the in-group to the world at large. So a spiritual education can also accomplish moral and religious education without moralizing or indoctrinating, as the architects of America knew. Precisely because of the partiality and even partisanship of religions, our devoutly Christian founding fathers refrained from building theirs into the state. Nothing fuels war so hotly as the word of God construed by the mind of man.

So in forbidding theocracy, the founding fathers certainly did not mean to bar spirituality from the government and education of this country. In addition to being Christians, they belonged to an international, ecumenical, cross-cultural spiritual brotherhood that was transmitting a universal esoteric teaching synthesized from Greek, Egyptian, Christian, Jewish, Persian, and Indian sources and common to all religions but driven underground by the exoteric, or popular, teaching that the ethnocentric majority exacted of its churches. Today Masons may seem as innocuous as Rotarians, but in the eighteenth century most of the great thinkers, scientists, artists, and leaders belonged to the lodges of Freemasonry, which did indeed inspire the American and French revolutions and played a major role in establishing modern democracy. Take out a dollar bill and look at the reverse of the U.S. seal—the esoteric side—and you will see the radiant eye, unfinished pyramid, and other devices of Freemasonry (Capt, 1979).

Like these emblems, the slogan on American coins—*e pluribus unum*—was drawn by the Freemasonic founding fathers from that universal spiritual tradition that ethnocentric people have interpreted as a history-long conspiracy against family, church, and state. Exoterically, the slogan refers to something like the union of the colonies or the immigration melting pot, both of which made one nation out of many peoples. Esoterically, it means that the many can become one because the many came from the One, a cosmic essence of which all partake. That is, plurality emanates from what is unity if spiritually perceived.

Always the one to take it on the chin, American schools have had to face most directly the dilemma of *e pluribus unum*—a single curriculum for a plural populace–without, I'm saying, the benefit of the *spiritual* half of this principle, stripped off by historians not conversant with, or embarrassed by, the esoteric teaching from which it came. A school book dispute shatters the shallow unity of the melting pot and forces the issue of how people who differ can harmoniously live together.

The real sin is exclusion. Spirituality is all-inclusive. Fundamentalism in both Christendom and Islam shows how ethnocentricity inverts religion precisely by excluding, which is also the very heart of censorship. Primitive perception confuses the race spirit with Spirit itself, the in-group with God.

Transmitting the Culture

In fending off the ethnicity of others, the book protesters were insisting on a principle that public schools seemed founded on—the transmission of culture. Fundamentalists are saying, "Those books are not passing on *our* heritage and values. They are indoctrinating our children with someone *else's* way of life." And indeed the educational goal of transmitting the culture always begs the question *Whose* culture? America is and always has been a pluralistic nation.

Even the thirteen original colonies could barely unite, they felt so different from one another, and the later waves of immigrants increased the cultural variety. School could still get by with a single curriculum for a plural populace so long as everyone wanted to be melted into the pot. But not today, when ethnic groups want to assert differences in order to salvage or consolidate an identity. How can a single curriculum serve a consitutuency when one faction of it abhors the same texts that another faction is outraged to find omitted?

Some people assert that America's problems come from having lost touch with the traditions and the values of the founding fathers and of Western civilization. They blame schools and families for not teaching the culture enough. But a culture is by definition self-transmitting. Every aspect of our society—from eating and mating habits to architecture and commerce—transmits the culture, not just Great Books and Great Works of Art, which are great because they have entered into the culture and influenced the lives of people who never even heard of them. People in "Western" culture are all part Platonic, Aristotelian, Augustinian, Newtonian, Darwinian, Freudian, and Einsteinian, no matter what their particular creeds, because these ways of perceiving are built into the society that they live and breathe in. Because it transmits itself out of school very effectively, though indirectly, one has to ask how much schools need to teach it and in which ways they can add to this self-transmission.

Actually, schools affect students far more in the way they operate than in what they intentionally teach. But this *way* partakes of the culture at least as much as the history, literature, and civics that are the conscious content. In other words, schools are transmitting the culture doubly—not only in what they explicitly teach about it but in how they go about the teaching itself. One is avowed, the other unavowed. This mixture of consciousness and unconsciousness means that schools are not only tranmitting the culture doubly but also double-mindedly, because their medium often contradicts their message.

Democracy is taught undemocratically. All while holding free enterprise and personal liberty before students as a great bequest to them from their cultural heritage, schools spoon-feed them through a doling system carefully programmed before their arrival that seldom allows them to make significant decisions, that in fact infantilizes them, and that has no equivalent in the society except mental hospitals, prisons, and nursing homes.

"Western" culture itself is self-contradictory. Plato and Aristotle represent two opposing philosophical approaches. Both Athenian and Jeffersonian democracy permitted slavery and forbade women to vote. Free enterprise and Marxism both came out of the same culture. Religion in the West runs the whole gamut of sacred to secular, from mysticism through the entire church spectrum to atheism. Even this conventional conception of "Western" civilization shows it to be pluralistic. It is made up of conflicting ideas, values, and practices.

But the school mission of transmitting the culture assumes that such knowledge constitutes a consistent moral framework and, furthermore, that it justifies the kind of society we have in America. Actually, Plato argued for censorship, and neither he nor Socrates approved of democracy. The Greek philosophers did advocate free inquiry, but Christianity has rarely permitted it and has frequently destroyed rival sects, both their members and their teachings. If schools were really meant to endow students with the Greek legacy, they would empower them to do the same free inquiry for which we so much value the Greek philosophers. Nothing could be farther from the case, and nothing could be more important for school reform than to deal with this discrepancy.

"Western" civilization is not a single set of values which, if we would only return to them, would by some sort of moral rearmament solve the problems we face. The fact is, it has built up both positive and negative forces that we must try to sort out and deal with (like Greek inquiry and Christian dogma). The major problems the world debates today are a big portion of "our heritage," created by the culture but not necessarily solvable by it. American society, for example, has granted personal freedom to its members but does not develop inner resources within individuals equal to this liberty, which too often becomes the freedom to hurt and be hurt. Free enterprise, for another example, has achieved the highest material standard of living but has resulted in a corporate private sector more powerful than government and therefore capable of holding the populace hostage as tyrannical governments did in the past.

A culture evolves, and it accretes and transforms past stages. This accounts for much of the pluralism and self-contradiction. The Romans built on the Greeks, and the Christians on the Romans, and so on. The accretions are transformed, but this does not result in a neat continuity with a summarizable conclusion that you can present honestly in school or college. Different epochs have concluded different things, and factions have differed in every epoch. In fact, if "Western" civilization has any defining characteristic it is diversity and disharmony—which is all right if acknowledged and dealt with as such.

On the growing edge of "Western" civilization, America, we can see another sort of pluralism than just the diversity of differing historical elements. The United States is not only a melting pot of different "Western" nationalities; it is a mosaic also of world civilizations. The native American Indian culture was here already, and settlers from Europe introduced into the country the black culture of slaves. Chinese laborers were imported in the nineteenth century to build railroads and service the gold-mining operations. Many immigrants, like Jews and Armenians, were not Christian or Western Christian. As a free country welcoming refugees, the U.S. made itself a multicultural nation. Today it includes a sizeable population of Asian and Middle Eastern people.

It also includes a whole spectrum of Hispanic people, who raise a central question for the educational goal of transmitting the culture. Latin Americans represent Western civilization to a degree, being Mediterranean Catholic, but are also part native Indian. In another way also, Latin American culture is not entirely "Western." Even the Spanish culture grafted onto the Indian contained strong Arabic and Islamic influences from the many centuries of Saracen occupation of Spain. When schools talk about transmitting the culture, they don't mean this Latin American culture—unless the majority of the local population is Mexican American or Puerto Rican and insists on it. They mean some more purely European version of "Western" culture. But even this will break down into various nationalities and churches—Polish or Irish, Protestant or Catholic. Appalachian fundamentalists resent the imposition on their children of mainstream urban Protestant culture.

So even if one were to accept a goal for schools of transmitting the culture, it is not at all clear except to jingoists what is meant by *culture.* Inevitably the definition simply comes down to what some majority or dominant subculture has in mind. Also, something as broad as "Western civilization" can be subdivided as finely as one likes, that is, right down to a sect or language or other ethnic body. One has only to look for examples to the strife among European immigrants, even as close as the British and the Irish, or between

Irish and Italian Catholics, not to mention between gringos and Chicanos, and fundamentalists and humanists.

This microscale concerns which peoples actually make up the school population today in the U.S. This is one way in which the question "*Whose* culture?" must be answered. After all, we can prate on all we want about "our Western heritage" and line up conventional European works into Great Books courses, but the culture really being transmitted in a given neighborhood is that of its local race, church, language, and ethnic group, many of whom can claim that the culture their schools are transmitting is not theirs but that of a remote majority. A hidden assumption about the population underlies both the *the* in "transmit the culture" and the *our* in "our heritage."

On a macro scale, culture is equally hard to define, because in reality civilizations merge, absorb each other, and at the very least influence each other. "Western" civilization is the artificial and ethnocentric creation of European scholars, who preferred to keep the roots of Greek culture north of the Mediterranean, in the family, and deny what the ancient world kept asserting, that Greek language, religion, and philosophy derived from Africa and the Middle East, from Semitic and Egyptian sources (See page 53). Great Books courses start with the Greeks and Jews, but that's an arbitrary cut-off point. Homer and Plato, St. Paul and Vergil were participating in cultural continuities preceding them by many centuries and reaching back into Egypt, Phoenicia, Persia, Chaldea, India, and the Far East. The more we know about older civilizations the more connected the world seems to have been. As one example, Socrates and Plato borrowed heavily from Pythagoras, who, it is well known, studied for decades abroad and underwent initiations in Egypt, Babylonia, Persia, and perhaps even India. Like the other "Indo-European" languages English is related to Sanskrit, and the all-important concept of 'zero' seems to have come from India via the Arabic world, not in time to serve Greek mathematics, which suffered all the limits of its absence.

Cultural traffic was heavy even before the Christian era between Europe, the Middle East, and the Far East. Some ideas, inventions, and practices have cycled among so many cultures that we'll probably never know which culture to credit for them. Cultures have always been constantly synthesizing themselves, as the tight interplay between Arabic Islam and Christian Europe shows during the

Crusades and the Moorish period of Spain. If schools were to convey the true pluralism of America's dominant culture, then minority peoples, such as blacks, Latin Americans, Asians, and Arabs, could rightly feel a part of it and identify with it, because they could see how their respective cultures have contributed to the majority culture they're immersed in.

The very pluralism of America, made increasingly apparent by minority self-assertion and new influxes of immigrants, has incited a backlash. Some Americans of European extraction who fear the country is being taken over by "foreigners" or is breaking up into ethnic pockets have recently refashioned the notion of "our heritage" into an educational movement calling for "cultural literacy." Proponents of this movement go so far as to list hundreds of facts and concepts that all school graduates ought to know in common. Actually, the insistence that all students learn a certain body of information for the sake of uniformity, far from being new, has always been one of the main curses of public schooling. Because it is arbitrary, boring, and trivial it alienates learners, fosters rote learning, and takes up undeserved space in the curriculum. Ultimately, the definition of culture for many parents comes down to "what I was taught as a child" and thus seriously limits the whole idea of education for their children.

The more immigrants pour into the United States and the larger grow the minority populations the louder sounds the cry for conformity to the majority culture. We're experiencing today a virtual panic of neonationalism. Factions in Florida and California, the states having the largest Hispanic populations, are lobbying to pass legislation declaring English the official language. "Whose country *is* this anyway, huh?" It seems that the nation will fall apart or fall into the wrong hands if schools don't soon homogenize everyone. Actually, immigrants and minorities tend to want most to fit in to the dominant culture, and mass media combine with franchise chains to do quite an efficient enough job of homogenizing a population. Making everyone's head alike, as schools also do, is a totalitarian way of achieving group unity. Conformity itself is the greater danger in a world that can be saved only by the creativity that comes from hybridism.

It is in this climate of nationalistic hysteria about losing identity that the old Great Books idea has resurged as part of "cultural literacy," that is, the mandatory teaching of someone's version of "our" heritage that can serve as a common medium of exchange, whether in the form of a lexicon or a canon. The real motive is to create an in-group for social solidarity, self-definition, and self-congratulation. Once again, chauvinism dominates at the expense of more basic human values. For educational purposes, it would be better for young people to grow up understanding the interconnectedness of all cultures, to learn not just about "our" culture but about all cultures at once, to examine not just "the" culture but culture, its very nature and how it affects us as individuals and how we affect it. Any culture both enables and cripples, and young people have to understand this.

To transmit a culture in school has been to retail it, that is, to overdistill it as history and social studies textbooks do for school children and as high school or college Great Books courses do through a chronological syllabus, starting with Homer and the Old Testament (already not very compatible!), and to spot-check the development of the civilization by sampling other representatives of later stages. Texts are highly selected, and lectures have to synopsize the rest. Any such effort to characterize either the West or America results in caricature, in all those stereotypes and buzzwords that anyone who learns more has to unlearn and that teach chauvinism as much as anything else.

Transmitting the culture through schools in such condensed and mandatory fashion has amounted to teaching ethnocentrism. It does not befit a democracy. It necessarily entails a kind of censorship, since it sets up a selective process for the curriculum that includes and excludes knowledge according to a preordained value system. It is not a moral nostrum for what ails a society. It is partial and partisan. It is not a whole enough and fair enough truth to stand as an educational goal of public schooling. It perpetuates ethnic conflict. A curriculum designed to melt pluralism and individualism down into a single people may have made some sense when America was consolidating itself into a nation, but today education must help youngsters resolve the self-contradictions that characterize both the culture and their own consciousness.

Advocates of "cultural literacy" and of other efforts to teach *our* heritage assume the same purpose for education as the fundamentalists, only they have a relatively broader notion of this heritage. The very concept of "Western" civilization is as parochial at Mortimer Adler's level of education as the Appalachian folk's concept is at its level. Both are ethnocentric.

The term "cultural literacy" implies something grand and important, whereas the culture is really betrayed by such shallow representation. Likewise, the term "literacy" falsely implies that the information is basic and necessary like reading and writing. By contrast, all students learn more, including about culture, if instead of requiring them to study the same things, the curriculum individualizes and pluralizes learning. As a defensive effort to enforce conformity to one idea of "our heritage," "cultural literacy" just dresses up the old blood-and-soil mentality in glamorous academic garb.

I am questioning that the transmission of culture should be the central goal of education. Not only does the whole society transmit the culture anyway, not only does schooling debase it in trying to synopsize and select for it in its overcontrolled way, but this very effort militates against another educational goal–open inquiry, learning to think for oneself—that, ironically, we attribute to our Western heritage. Here we are double-minded too: you can't program curriculum to make sure all students learn the same corpus of knowlege and still expect them to learn to think for themselves. By itself, transmitting culture builds ethnocentricity, which is the ultimate obstacle to mental and spiritual growth.

Cultural Censorship

Transmitting any heritage entails selecting some ideas, frameworks, and values and excluding others. Exclusion is built into the very idea of education as cultural transmission. How much difference is there between prohibiting certain facts and ideas and simply omitting them? In other words, how far does the selectivity of this sort of education have to go before *it* becomes censorship? When creek preachers try to control reading, that's called censorship. When sleek academics do it, it's called cultural literacy.

Censorship takes many forms. Cultural bias so pervades our thinking that we're too unaware of what is being included and excluded to regard this selectivity as kin to censorhip, which receives attention as a *revolt.* Never, for example, have I seen mentioned in books on American history for either school or the general public the fact that the majority of the signers of the Declaration of Independence, the members of the Continental Congress, the officers in the Continental Army were Freemasons, as were George Washington, Benjamin

Franklin, and Paul Revere who were heads of Masonic lodges. From its framework of universalist spirituality, freemasonry supplied the founding fathers with the social ideals of liberty, equality, and fraternity, along with such fitting mottoes and symbols as I referred to earlier. It also enabled the upstart nation to win the support of fellow Masons abroad, like Lafayette, and of France itself, where Franklin was made head of the Nine Sisters Lodge while ambassador there lobbying for aid against England. So devoted was the brotherhood to its ideals that high-ranking Masons right in the English establishment put these ideals before their own country and aided the United States (Faÿe, 1935).

Does this colossal omission confirm the fundamentalists' countercharge that a secular humanist establishment has done much censoring of its own? A secretive organization that rivaled the church in spiritual appeal and that subordinated patriotism to universal justice was bound to become a target for censorship by both religious and secular factions. On the one hand, it was transmitting the cross-cultural esoteric traditions that Christians had anathematized earlier; on the other hand, it was implementing the eighteenth-century Enlightenment of Voltaire and the Encyclopedists (who were all Freemasons). In all the flag waving and prattle about the American way, the real story of how democracy came about remains censored. The modern secular establishment doesn't want America's birth associated with this mystical fraternity any more than the church does.

In fact science has taken over from religion the role of censor. As the Inquisition was dying out during the Renaissance, scientists began to strip off metaphysics and humanities from both math and science with the result that today they seem strange and inhuman, difficult to learn. The founders of modern science themselves—Newton, Bacon, and Descartes—drew much of their perception from the esoteric traditions, as transmitted then, for example, by the Rosicrucians, the immediate predecessors of Freemasons.

These older ties to esoteric traditions embarrass today's scientific establishment, which avoids referring to the writings of their founders that show this powerful "prescientific" influence and which claims instead that modern science developed only in the measure that it shook free of such traditions. The scientific establishment's literal reading, for example, of the highly symbolic texts of alchemy and astrology, which Newton took very seriously, compares to fundamentalist interpretation of the equally symbolic Christian scriptures. Adding its own inquisition to the church's has very effectively censored out of our present civilization a vital metaphysical force that would render contemporary problems more intelligible and would contribute exactly what is needed to solve these problems.

The fundamentalists are wrong to invent a religion of secular humanism and a science of creationism just to try to turn the First Amendment around in their favor, but they are right that science is not taught hypothetically enough. Nobody really understands electromagnetism, which is just a pragmatic term for some apparently related observations. Students should not walk off thinking that science is definitive, materialistic fact, unrelated to philosophy and metaphysics, when in fact the entities that theoretical physicists talk about are as hard to see, believe, and understand as the medieval theological conceits that we have learned to laugh at. Though at the other end of the intellectual scale from fundamentalists, today's Theosophists and Rosicrucians consider Darwinism as a narrowly physical theory of evolution that while true enough so far as it goes lacks the cosmological framework that would best explain the facts by subsuming them into a more comprehensive concept of evolution.

Commercial Censorship

To tell the truth, I worry less about book banners and book burners than I do about book *publishers*. I mean the publishers of trade books for the general public, not just textbooks for schools. As profit corporations, they have far greater power to limit what I can read than any special-interest group. I can hear about and probably still get hold of a book that has been banned or burned, but I will never know about the worthy manuscripts that never became books at all because publishers deemed them not profitable enough. Counting newspapers and magazines, movies and other media, the communications companies have consolidated through mergers as much as or perhaps more than any other industry. Publishers have not only been taken over by each other but by mixed conglomerates. According to the 1990 edition of *Writer's Market,* "2% of U. S. publishers are putting out 75% of the titles" (p. 47).

What and who can get published are shrinking rapidly all the time in the United States as publishers and distributors go more and more only for big sellers. Formerly, acquisitions editors chose which manuscripts to publish according to mixed criteria by which they could accept worthy or important books of moderate readerships as well as the potboilers that would in effect subsidize them. The job of the marketing people was to find ways to sell their choices. Today this has reversed. The marketing staff usually tells the editors what to select according to their knowledge of what sells best, which is in turn determined largely by distributors as monopolistic as the publishers themselves. Three or four large bookstore chains retail most of the trade books sold in the United States and hence establish the marketing criteria that publishers look for in selecting manuscripts. Publishers feel they have to choose manuscripts to fit these successful market categories while also avoiding books that may take a long time to pay for themselves, because tax laws no longer exempt publishers' inventories.

At the same time, these major publishers have quit screening general trade manuscripts for themselves. Just as they discovered that too much competition was bad for business, they realized that by considering submissions only from agents they could shift the expense of screening from themselves to the authors, who pay agents, and never have to bother with any manuscripts except the most likely candidates for best sellers, since that's about all the agents are screening for, their criteria having narrowed along with those of editors and retailers. It is difficult to get a manuscript read even by an agent, because they too won't bother with unsolicited manuscripts but rather sift for big winners by requiring outlines or samples first. They don't want ten or fifteen percent of a book that may sell just moderately well.

The search for the blockbuster sellers has reached the point that the industry focuses almost entirely on what is well known and proven—certain topics, certain treatments, or certain people. The big publishers believe in lots of insurance. So huge numbers of books are about how to put on weight and how to take it off—cookbooks and diet books—or by celebrities whose names will ensure a big seller whatever the content or quality of what they write. A celebrity need not necessarily be a famous author but a politician, entertainer, sports hero, or criminal—anyone so long as the name has achieved notoriety and thus already done the advertising in advance. Even well known products are featured in a book so that promotion can be tied in with the manufacturer and the book cross-advertised with the product. When publishers do accept worthy books not deemed to be good sellers, they promote them so little and spend so much instead on their hot items that they in fact prove right their own marketing judgment, and so the cycle turns over again. These self-fulfilling prophecies are not really prophetic but historical, since they are based on past successes. In a 1991 article in *The Nation* titled "The Paperbacking of Publishing," Ted Solotaroff described from an editor's viewpoint these "conditions that drive an editor to double his standards and join the hunt for commercial books. What used to be called selling out is today simply a strategy for surviving" (p. 403).

This reliance on the tried and true to maximize profit is rendering big publishing virtually impenetrable to the really original minds and creative ideas that alone will solve the mounting problems of the world. We will feel this loss more and more as we struggle in vain to make failing old ways work. Unquestionably, manuscripts are being turned down today of a sort that would have been published in the past, even a few years ago, and that will be sorely needed in the future. Of course, this very restriction plus new flexibility in printing technology have engendered many small publishers who do take in some of these manuscripts, but they are part of the 98 percent of publishers collectively reaching only 25 percent of the reading public. In other words, worthy and original manuscripts *may* find an outlet but can reach only a few hundred or a few thousand readers.

The most fanatic censors could not wreak damage of this magnitude. For its equal we have to look back to when Romans and Christians and Saracens took turns burning the libraries of Alexandria, before the power to control what people read passed from theocracies to private enterprise. A society that leaves the dissemination of ideas to such ungovernably selfish organizations as today's corporations is begging for trouble and foolish enough to deserve what happens as a result. An old-fashioned despot might well sneer that the private sector to which his powers were so idealistically transferred abuses the citizenry just as much as he ever did.

Profit corporations constitute the other part of the private sector that now enjoys, along with various religious and secular factions, the powers of tyranny formerly reserved to government. Corporations are the most powerful part of the private sector because government has neither the legal nor financial means to control them.

They have become so large and wealthy that they can easily overwhelm whatever agencies are supposed to regulate them and even buy off the legislators who create the agencies, especially when they band together as they do against not only government regulation but against consumers and workers as well, in mockery of the old capitalistic competitive open market.

Both education and publication act as censors by closing down the range of thought while trying to do something else, one to solidify the society and the other to make money. But their sorts of censorship wreak devastation far worse than that of some bands of zealots and bigots who have set out to limit thought deliberately. Both schools and publishers exclude too much. Managers of corporations have got to identify more broadly with the rest of society, so that they see themselves as having other functions than maximizing profits. School constituencies must identify more broadly with other societies and with the rest of nature.

Spiritualizing Education

Democracy is not of course supposed to produce such tyrannies as thought control, but so long as individuals broaden their freedom but not their identity along with it, then their special-interest groups will exclude and violate each other until they invert democracy itself. The founding fathers were assuming a spiritual framework for personal liberty and free enterprise that alone can make them work. In the midst of our pluralism we have to feel our oneness. Otherwise, individuals and corporations think so narrowly that they thwart one another's rights as badly as despots. This prompts some people to call for a return to central conformity, just the sort of escape from freedom that, in his book by that title, Erich Fromm (1941) so brilliantly showed to explain the rise of Hitler and other modern dictators.

The real solution to social disintegration is to develop the individual even further, to continue the evolution of freedom inward until mental liberation matches political liberation. This requires breaking through the social boundaries that restrict knowing and thinking—expanding consciousness beyond the limitations of any particular family, church, or state to a universal identity—the only way to have peaceful families, churches, and states. (As the seventeenth-century poet Richard Lovelace wrote, "I could not love thee, dear, so much, / Loved I not honor more.") Otherwise there is coherence only *within* a group but not *across* groups.

Paradoxically, as people develop inner strength, they draw closer to others farther away, because they rely less on those around them and seek bonds based less on blood and soil than on common humanity. And common divinity. "Everything that rises must converge." The American Transcendentalists provide an inspiring model. They were the most individualistic people our culture has produced, but they identified the most universally. Thoreau's refusal to pay taxes seems antisocial, but actually he did so to protest the war to annex part of Mexico. That is, he placed the greater social cohesion over the lesser.

I think fundamentalists are right to hold out for spiritual education, but I think that cannot come about by controlling reading matter or by teaching morality and religion as such. They are right too that our secular society tends to censor out *spirituality* in its distrust of *religion*.

But education can be spiritual without manipulating minds, without teaching Spirituality 101 replete with textbooks, lectures, and midterms (open to qualified juniors and seniors only). In fact, I think schools will become spiritual only in the measure they *reduce* manipulation. Some of it—the overcontrolling of texts and topics and of the situations in which reading and writing occur—is designed to direct thought where adults think it should go. Some of the manipulation—the obsessive testing and the military-industrial managerial systems—is just bureaucratic self-accommodation. Some is state control over both teachers and students. One way or another, in the name of "structure," youngsters are infantilized. We can't expect them to understand democracy when most of what they have seen is tyranny.

The first step toward spiritual education is to put students in a stance of responsible decision-making and in an unprogrammed interaction with other people and the environment. As part of this change I would drop textbooks in favor of trade books, a syllabus in favor of a classroom library, and go strongly for individual and small-group reading. Any specific presenting and sequencing of texts, whether done in the editorial offices of amoral corporations or within the somewhat more sanctified walls of the faculty conference room, short-circuits the learning process and undermines the will of the student.

Creek preachers aren't the only ones afraid of reading and writing. We all are, and that is the real reason they have proved inordinately difficult to teach. Literacy *is* dangerous and has always been so regarded. It naturally breaks down barriers of time, space, and culture. It threatens one's original identity by broadening it through vicarious experiencing and the incorporation of somebody *else's* hearth and ethos. So we feel profoundly ambiguous about literacy. Looking on it as a means of transmitting our culture to our children, we give it priority in education, but recognizing the threat of its backfiring we make it so tiresome and personally unrewarding that youngsters won't want to do it on their own, which is of course when it becomes dangerous. They will read only when big people make them—a teacher or some other boss down the line.

The net effect of this ambivalence is to give literacy with one hand and take it back with the other, in keeping with our contradictory wish for youngsters to learn to think but only about what we already have in mind for them. The overcontrol of reading texts and writing topics that is meant to make literacy only a one-way transmitter is of course precisely what keeps us from teaching it successfully. I joke that school consists of one year of beginning reading and eleven years of remedial reading. This *is* an absurd state of affairs, but it is a societal problem going beyond schools alone to the universal fear of literacy based on ethnocentricity and the educational goal of transmitting the culture.

The solution to censorship may also be the way to a spiritual education. A single course of reading for a pluralistic populace doesn't make sense unless we really do want a cookie-cutter curriculum. If students are routinely reading individually and in small groups, negotiating different reading programs with the teacher, parents, and classmates, no family can object that their child is being either subjected to or barred from certain books or ideas. Teachers and librarians can point out skewed reading fare in conferring with students and parents and can keep students and books constantly circulating. Students read far more, it is well known, when they read in this fashion, which means that they will read more of everything—including the classics. At Phillips Exeter Academy, where I once taught, the faculty could agree to teach classics but couldn't agree on which classics. What we did agree on was a kind of education that would so sensitize students that whenever they should later fetch up against a classic without being told, they would be able to spot it for themselves. A spiritual education subtilizes the sensibility so that whatever finer realities there may be within us and within the universe we may detect.

As We Identify, So We Know

Pluralism must be central to future schooling, because both spiritual and mental growth depend on widening the identity. Every social system is a knowledge system and has limitations that must be overcome. Both learning to think and rejoining the All require expanding the frequency spectrum to which we can attune. Great books, yes, but youngsters need to experience *all* kinds of discourse and all kinds of voices and viewpoints and styles—to hear out the world. Our heritage, okay, but we need to encompass *all* heritages, to cross cultures, raise consciousness enough to peer over the social perimeters that act as parameters of knowledge. The Kanawha County imbroglio taught me that the same attachments to blood and soil, hearth and ethos, that Christ so vividly enjoined us not to put before Him, work against intellectual understanding as well as spiritual development. As we identify, so we know. That is how spirituality develops the mind. As we know, so we identify. That is how the mind develops spirituality.

But our selves and very lives depend, we feel, on localized identifications with the family, neighborhood, ethnic group, church, nation, and language. We have an investment in not knowing anything that will disturb these identifications. So we tend to limit what we are willing to know to what is known and accepted in our reference group. I call this not wanting to know "agnosis," partly to contrast it with "gnosis," the esoteric term for direct and total revelation, but partly also to create an analogy with clinical states like anesthesia, amnesia, and aphasia. Just as our inner system may block sensory perception or memories or abstraction, our acculturation may block any knowledge from within or without that threatens these identities. Agnosis is self-censorship.

One generation of teachers has somehow got to bring through one generation of students who will have thoughts we have not had before. It is clear that the nation's and the planet's problems cannot be solved by just thinking along the lines we do now according to our heritage. Societies relying on conventional wisdom are doomed. They need instead some breathtakingly new ideas that will never come from a cookie-cutter curriculum designed just to relay some gist of what is known and thought now. The next generation must have an education creative enough to survive its inheritance. No country still ransoming its education to nationalistic competition and ethnocentricity will survive. If we don't enable the young to transform the culture, we won't have one to transmit.

The world is riven right and left because the various cultures strive so intently to perpetuate themselves that they end by imposing themselves on one another. These lethal efforts to make others like oneself burlesque the expanded identity that would make possible real global unity. The secret of strife is that groups *need* enemies to maintain definition, because differences define. The exclusivity of cultures is so dangerous that each must build into itself the means of transcending itself. Actually, I think the deepest spiritual teachings in all cultures have tried to do this but in doing so seemed subversive, which is why they had to go underground (where historians rarely find them).

Practically, this means deconditioning ourselves, jumping cultures, slipping outside the cage of mere genetic and environmental inheritance. Schools must become places where people relate to each other and the rest of nature as all one. If we know as we identify, then the more broadly we identify the more we will know. If social systems are knowledge systems, then to know the most, join the broadest social system. Become a citizen of the universe. Educate to liberate.

If we construed public education as personal liberation, it would hardly mean more than fulfilling the already professed goal of teaching the young to think for themselves. But truly free inquiry has conflicted so much with the old goal of cultural transmission and identity maintenance that we have sabotaged our own noble aim. This is unnecessary and unwise. If we educate youngsters to transcend their heritage, they will be able to transform it and lead other cultures to do the same. The American way is to pioneer. And the practical way is the spiritual way.

Part 2

Wanting to Know

The point of investigation is to find out something new. But what is new to one individual or social group is not to another. Also, whether some finding is regarded as new even by a single individual or group may depend considerably on the form and the context it appears in—or on who says so. Maybe the *notion* of some knowledge, the *possibility* of its being true, is not new, but its confirmation or acceptance might be. If the validating of new knowledge involves considerable social negotiation, then we can certainly expect this to be even more true in order for this knowledge to be communally acted upon.

Researchers are in the position of trying to investigate the same physical, psychological, social, and cultural environments that determine the nature and conditions of their research itself. To be of any great use to education in the future, research must rise to a new sophistication in the kind of self-examination that we are familiar with, for example, in literary criticism. Like textual interpretation, research needs to undergo a kind of deconstruction. Just as the contexts of the author, text, and reader must be taken into account in dealing with the meaning of a text, so must the circumstances of the investigator, the project, and the applier of the findings in making sense of research. What are the personal and cultural subtexts of the research report? Just as current hermeneutics penetrates well beyond the truism that people read into a text some of their own inner life, and that authors say more than they realize, this new self-examination should far exceed the mere reminder that any research is vulnerable to bias. As much as schooling itself, the research informing public education needs reform also.

Drawbacks of Traditional Research

Research is a kind of rhetoric, one among many ways of persuading. Our society seems to revere scientific research but actually ignores its findings when some other rhetoric better matches social motives. In education, for example, research results are used to justify traditional teaching practices far more than to innovate, for which less motivation exists. Thus literature and art have been taught as history and criticism, not for reasons inherent in the arts or in learning psychology but because the schematizing that history and criticism impose on a field format it to fit academic modes of operating, including research procedures. Formal grammatical analysis has for many years defied research indicating that it does not improve speaking or writing but displaces activities that do. Business and government were implementing the research on the effectiveness of small groups decades before schools ever considered "collaborative learning," which is still making its way into public education only with great difficulty. Most directions of curricular reform proposed in all subjects today could have been begun far earlier had both practical evidence and research results played a major role in determining public education.

Rationally, findings about how people learn and function should exert great influence on curriculum and methods, but they do not. Tests, textbooks, and college entrance requirements determine curriculum far more. But aren't these themselves based on research? Rather, even when findings do affect education via these three, they are impressed into the service of social, political, and economic factions vying to influence schooling to their advantage or persuasion.

Research lends itself to partisanship because on the big educational issues the findings are often opposed or inconclusive. In the supersensitive field of reading, for example, authoritative researchers summarize findings very differently. Barak Rosenshine and Robert Stevens (1984) conclude that children learn to read better in a strongly teacher-centered program of small steps, constant monitoring, and teacher-run small groups, whereas Roger Farr (1981, 1986) concludes that student-centered activities emphasizing the personal feelings of the learner work best. Significantly, Farr was much influenced by Kenneth Goodman (an advisor on his summary) and Frank Smith—strong advocates of independent, naturalistic learning—whereas Rosenshine and Stevens don't even mention Goodman and Smith in their extensive bibliography. This sort of selectivity points up how easily one may use research to justify a position on learning of the greatest importance.

Especially as educational research is an applied science, we have to consider the circular ways in which it interacts with the society that sponsors it. First, university-based people usually do the research, some of which is conducted *in* schools as well as *for* schools. It draws on general or "pure" research in the behavioral sciences, as in cognition or child development, to the extent that findings there help make decisions about how to proceed pedagogically. But to bridge the gap between that research and practice, educators or social scientists may conduct experiments in school itself, commonly "intervention research" to find out if changing the way something is taught will improve results.

School research is tremendously limited by which practices schools will permit. A lot of findings just show these limits themselves, not what might best occur. Even innovative experiments prove little. Either it's not possible to control all the variables in such a multifarious setting well enough to convince decision makers to initiate change, or institutional climate and routines dilute the innovation in the direction of convention. So many factors are at play both in school and in students' lives outside that it is extremely difficult to ascribe failure or success to the particular conditions of the experiment. And any really serious change in learning practices or conditions seems to put some students at risk as guinea pigs. The worse off the school performance, however, the less there is to lose and the more risk can be taken. So the most drastic experiments tend to occur among poor and minority students already regarded as "at risk." Changes are apt to be made in these cases less on the soundness of research findings than on the principle that it can't hurt to try something else. Although comparisons of methods using actual student populations would seem to be the most effective form of educational research, in fact attitudes more than science will determine both the outcome of comparisons that may be attempted and the changes that may, with or without the research, eventually take place.

Partly to control variables better, and partly just for practical teaching purposes, experimental school research has zeroed in on piecemeal activities and thus created another grave danger. No research that reports success in one area of language learning should be enacted into curriculum without knowing other effects of the procedure tested. Much serious damage is done by forcing results—usually short-lived—for one highly targeted skill at the expense of other, often more important components in thought and language or overall personal development. Scores resulting from a certain specific teaching practice can look very good if you don't look also at the price paid for them in the total learning picture.

But controlling for unintended effects is rarely built into experimental design and indeed would in most cases be impossible because too many effects are unforeseeable and widely scattered across the mental life. And since every segregated-skill experiment does similar damage, together they add up to an intolerable price—the betrayal of the real goals of, say, speaking, reading, writing, and thinking for the sake of ensuring periodic "progress" in the subskills alleged to comprise them.

Again trying to offset the frustrations of school research, investigators have focused considerably on how adult or proficient practitioners go about an activity targeted in school, such as reading or writing. How does the novice become an adept? Triangulating school experimentation, knowledge of child development, and observation of skilled performers does indeed seem a necessary way to piece together some practical understanding of how to teach. In reflecting on the "fragmented, staccato nature" of the history of reading research, the highly regarded learning researcher Richard L. Venezky (1984) observes first that today's research favors the parts of reading so much over the whole act of reading as to be of little help in teaching. Then he says, "But even if the studies being done today were directed toward an improved understanding of reading, a chasm between research results and reading instruction would remain. First, adults and not children are the favored subjects for most of the studies now being reported on reading processes" (p. 27). I myself have felt that some of the psycholinguistic findings about how adults read have been too readily translated into learning processes for children, with the result that the oral mediation between speech and print that learners need to rely on has been downplayed on grounds that expert readers bypass oracy and directly connect text to thought. Though an understandable effort to bridge from this more reliable research to school practice, extrapolating backward from the second-nature proficiency of the adept to the initial learning of the novice has added to the confusion and contention in a field already too notorious for both.

Venezky goes on to make another observation worth keeping in mind during any deliberations about educational research. "Second, investigations on learning processes do not within themselves answer instructional questions. . . . Perhaps Henry James (1901) was correct when he said 'You make a great, a very great mistake, if you think that psychology, being the science of mind's laws, is something from which you can deduce programmes and schemes and methods of instruction for immediate schoolroom use. Psychology is a science, and teaching is an art, and sciences never generate arts directly out of themselves' " (pp. 27–28).

For their part, universities pose problems as obdurate for educational research as do schools. For career advancement, academicians are expected to make a "contribution to knowledge" and to publish it (or perish). This puts enormous pressure on researchers to produce and to produce fast—in time for that doctorate, appointment, promotion, or grant. Under these conditions, we can't expect most research to be significant. Indeed, research findings in education rarely reveal anything we didn't already know.

For example, Roger Farr, in his summary of reading research cited earlier, writes, "What, then, can we say about the teaching of reading after 80 years and over 12,000 investigations?" He answers that (1) it "should involve children in experiences that they enjoy and that demonstrate [what reading can do for them]"; (2) "the more closely skill-drill exercise is associated with a student's personal reasons for reading, the more likely such exercise is to develop readers"; and (3) the program should be "geared to the interests and needs of *individual* children . . . [including] many types of reading on many topics at a variety of appropriate readability levels" (p. 20). Should we really be flabbergasted by these findings? Pertinence, personal interest, and involvement are just three points making the same commonsense point that the best learning is individualized and pluralistic. Who needs to wait on research for such "data"?

This is the pattern. When I look at research in writing, which has received much more attention in recent years, I find there too that what seems to excite researchers are findings about human truths that we know already—or should know if we're paying any attention at all to children and to our own social and mental processes. Here are some research revelations excerpted from an excellent synopsis by two leading investigators of learning to write (Dyson and Freedman, 1991):

- Children "control first-order systems, like speech and drawing, before they control second-order systems, like written language. . . . "
- Children "play with print's basic graphic features, for example, its linearity and the arrangement of print lines upon the page . . . . "
- Children's writings "undergo transformations during the school years" in the direction of greater length, structural complexity, and internal coherence.
- "Children seem willing to change spelling and handwriting earlier than they do structure and content" and "may find little use for revision unless they are grappling with ordering of ideas . . . . "
- More expert writers allow more for their audience than less expert writers.
- The composing of adult writers consists of "several main processes—planning, transcribing text, reviewing" that occur recursively as needed.
- Composing is a "hierarchically organized, goal-directed, problem-solving process."
- When "writers see their topics as more abstract, they spend more time planning," and they "tend to pause more when writing pieces that require generalizations than when writing reports." (pp. 760–65)

I suspect that virtually any educated layman could have predicted these findings, if asked about each point, on the basis of observing either how people write out of school or children's general behavior, of experience reading texts of varying maturity, and of general understanding about such gradients as concrete to abstract and subjective to objective. It is true that research reassures us of what we know, formulates this more precisely, collates examples, and marshals evidence for argument. These are all important psychologically and socially, but it's important too to understand precisely the nature and value of this sort of research.

I don't mean to disparage the work of the responsible, intelligent investigators who are accumulating such findings. If research turns up so little really new knowledge, I think that's for systemic reasons going well beyond the personal qualities of individual researchers to cultural, political, and economic forces that work their effects on schools and universities. Their institutionalism so depersonalizes learning that we dissociate personal knowledge from professional life and pretend not to know, in effect, or truly lose touch with our experiential understanding of how we function.

Let's pursue the university setting in which educational researchers operate. For one thing, there are simply too many academic people trying to advance their careers for very much of the research ever to make a real contribution to knowledge. In order to be sure of ascertaining some data definite enough and soon enough to earn that degree or that rank, the goal of the research must be too clear and the scope of it too small. Even well established investigators have to operate within funding terms intended to yield clear-cut results in a short time, because the administrators of funding institutions also must quickly prove themselves, like CEOs of profit corporations making those quarterly reports look good. The insignificance of much research stems rather directly from this short-term managerial mentality, which infects all of business and government, where administrators with real decison-making powers characteristically move after short terms in office. A researcher sets out to prove something already pretty sure to be true, for which evidence can pretty surely be adduced in time for the quick payoff. So if the findings are not obvious, they are trivial.

A truism that hardly anyone seriously doubts may be formally proved and thus technically counted as a contribution to knowledge. Often the "finding" will be pronounced in new terms, however, and the old truth renamed so that it appears as a revelation. Since previous practitioners and researchers may well have accepted or assumed this truth for some time, investigators sometimes have to use fresh terminology to try to patent their finding, carve out some professional turf to which their name can be affixed.

Now, a systemic problem like this can be allowed for by those who are well aware of it, but most lay people and no doubt some researchers themselves don't really understand that the new knowledge is not new, at least not in some quarters and in some terms. This is not harmless, because assuming that a finding is new when it is not confuses one's thinking. "If this is new, then it must be different from such-and-such, which I have always known but which must be something else." Or "I did not know this before because research has only now disclosed it." The researcher's need, as it were, to copyright something in the public domain may in this way cause the consumers of research to deny they knew something previously or to dissociate their knowledge from the new "findings." They give credence to professional researchers over their own knowledge making.

This is exactly what happens to students all through school. Of course schools do furnish them some facts they really didn't know, but by formatting and formulating information in unfamiliar jargon, they make it extremely difficult for students to seam in from what they do know (which varies with each student) to what they are truly learning for the first time. It is critical for people to build on old perceptions and understandings, to keep transforming these as they learn really new things. But they must know what it is they already know and not discount their own knowledge in deference to an authority asserting, "You didn't know this until I told you."

Ironically, one of the findings most bruited about today tells us that children actively *construct* knowledge by transforming old understanding as they assimilate new information into it (Resnick, 1987). But this depends on knowing and honoring fully what they already know. This finding itself is now utilized in school reform to support "active" (!) learning, student empowerment, and student centering, which is fine, but had schools and universities not treated us all as inert manipulables all those years, we would not be so astonished to discover that people build their own knowledge structures by actively putting together as best they can whatever information and understanding the environment makes available. Had we *let* children learn, set up an authentic knowledge-making environment not dictated by tests, textbooks, and political and institutional controls, every school would have been a natural laboratory in which we could have learned some really new things. Instead, for example, we learned only about school- and university-induced impediments to literacy until learning results were so terrible that we finally started looking at how people read and write in circumstances that *are* real, outside of school.

In short, most educational research merely rips away the veils from understanding obscured by our learning institutions themselves. It is a form of permitting ourselves to know what we ourselves have suppressed. Such research serves a needed purpose. But let's be clear about what that role is and about what sense of *new* is true of research that gives us back to ourselves.

Let's take two important ideas that appear to have come from research but that observant teachers and parents have long known. One is the truth that the language used in many homes differs considerably from the way language is used in school and that consequently children coming from some homes will have a much harder time learning in school than those coming from homes more like those of the teachers. Researchers began to proclaim this during the 1960s, when the United States started to acknowledge the right of minorities to assert their identities and their differences, but minority children and families certainly knew this all along, and teachers were dealing with it, well or badly, all the time. What was new was a political change in society that permitted such truths to be acknowledged and acted upon. All research did besides document this old knowledge in some linguistic and cognitive detail was to *officially promulgate and validate it.*

Often the documentation took the form of anecdotal evidence and case histories—ethnographic research—differing only in degree of formalization from stories that children, parents, and teachers had long been telling, or could have been telling had someone cared to elicit their experience. Finally, society cared enough to ask. It was not that these discrepancies in language use were not known, and even complained or joked about, but that *academicians* didn't know about them or didn't bother to examine the details of these obvious ethnic and socioeconomic differences—not until more minority and rural people started becoming academicians themselves. To *whom* is this knowledge new? Or in what state of mind is this new knowledge?

The other example is the notion of multiple intelligences. With all due credit to the sensitive and much needed *attention* that Howard Gardner has given to this, most people have always understood that human beings function through more than discursive intelligence, that they know and cognize through their senses, their feelings, and their bodies. Again, it may be *academic* people who have least known this, because they make a living mostly through verbal and logical knowledge. But no one needs research to tell them that some other kinds of intelligences are operating when people compose music and choreography, paint and sculpt, act, sail a boat, or grow corn. The knowledge of multiple intelligences was not new, at least to large parts of the society, but this knowledge was not welcome or implemented in education because schools were socially and politically too committed to discursive learning that aped the university. After school reform became a serious issue, *then* the knowledge was allowed.

In both examples, research "discovered" what the society was now willing to permit its schools to deal with. In this sense, research removed a bias that denied we knew what we knew and thus acted as an offical license to *implement* this old knowledge, which we will still probably not accomplish for a long time yet.

Actually, research about the methodology of reading and writing has never been necessary but has only seemed so because of the unnatural learning conditions that schools have imposed on children. As research is now "showing," the more schools approximate the authentic reading and writing circumstances in which literacy is practiced outside of school, the more they succeed. Only societal forces to the contrary, mainly for purposes of institutional and ideological control, ever prevented our seeing this obvious way of proceeding in the first place. *How* to teach reading and writing is a red herring, since we have always known what these authentic reading and writing circumstances are in the home or workplace, and since we can learn what else we need to know by observing children in comparable circumstances. The concept of teachers as their own researchers would have been part of good schooling generations ago had curriculum and methods not been dictated from beyond the classroom via tests, textbooks, and various regulations and requirements up the line. Teachers' ongoing investigation of what is or is not happening among their students is an intrinsic part of good teaching and should not have to wait on or depend on professional researchers to come in and formalize it.

No, the real need for research is not to find a methodology for teaching literacy, which was always there whenever students and teachers should be freed to engage in it, but to understand the place of literacy in an overall learning program for today's stage of evolution in culture and consciousness. This requires a shift in the nature of how research is conducted.

The recent shift from experimental and statistical research toward ethnography represents a positive effort to demythologize academic research, and still get academic credit, by honoring and sharpening how we learn all the time as observers and participants. Ethnography, case histories, teacher journals can document in more detail what we think we know, adjust and refine it, focus and raise to public forum what is personally known, and perhaps aid in seeing how to institute in schools those authentic conditions in which literacy and other human activities are learned out of school. As an antidote to the artificiality of manipulative schooling, ethnography at least focuses educators on realistic ways of learning occurring out of school that may be brought into school.

But if the real goal of research is *surprise*—truly new knowledge—ethnography too suffers from the small-scope, short-term framework and the societal biases that limit other types of research. Investigators work best when enabled to pursue a major learning issue for a long time and to draw on many disciplines and cultures. Multicultural, interdisciplinary teams of investigators probably work best of all, if freed of professional shibboleths and institutional politics. Another late disclosure of educational research has been the efficacy of "collaborative learning," especially when focused on "projects." The same authoritarian institutionalism and individual competition that prevented educators from knowing enough to implement cooperative small-group process in schools a long time ago has also impeded *researchers* from framing investigation in knowledge networks capacious enough to discover things we really did not know before.

What educational research needs is a more comprehensive perspective, a more pluralistic cross-referencing of knowledge, as I will attempt to envision now. Otherwise we do not know what to make of, or what to do with, even good research with authentic discursive activities, because we don't understand well enough the relationships among the various thinking and verbalizing faculties to know what we are doing in working with any one of them, such as comprehending or composing. Besides practical literacy, finally, what in the bigger picture of individual and social life are we really trying to accomplish through language? Ultimate values must enter into any thoughtful overview of present and future. For all these reasons, literacy and literature, like other kinds of knowledge, are best discussed in constant relation to culture and consciousness.

Beyond Materialism

In their efforts to make their disciplines as "hard" as those in the natural sciences, behavioral scientists have often taken on a scientific swagger that, interestingly, the physicist has been forced to drop. The harder the science the harder does the scientist run up against the limits of the scientific method. After Einstein's relativity and Heisenberg's uncertainty have come other principles, like that of probability, to attenuate and qualify the realities of matter. The more one views holistically, from multiple vantage points and expanded perspectives, the more relativistically one thinks. As the interplay of "particles" in a nucleus dissipates the very idea of a particle, the meaning of a single text extends out across the whole network of reciprocally defining words and cross-referring intertextuality that makes up signification for writer and reader. If both literature and physics operate today on a principle of relativity, behavioral scientists should be able to drop the defensive effort to pretend their disciplines are "hard."

Within this framework of new self-awareness, the subject matter of research should be drastically and daringly enlarged. It remains far too physical, partly in allegiance to a lingering behaviorism and partly in adherence to an old-fashioned doctrine of nineteenth-century positivism, according to which nothing is real that can't be hefted, counted, or perceived by the senses. In an era when theoretical physics sounds stranger than scholastic theology, and the most important "things" in science are mathematical constructs, this materialism seems inappropriate indeed. Researchers have got to quit intimidating each other by disparaging attempts to explore the intangible—especially when investigating the mental life! The old positivistic scientism has created a climate we still live in which I call the "scientific inquisition," whereby the research establishment punishes its members for dealing with taboo subjects, as the church did before it.

The Body Electric: Electromagnetism and the Foundation of Life (Becker and Selden, 1985) not only gives an account of orthopedic surgeon Robert Becker's pioneering experimentation on the healing power of electricity but also makes of this research a case history of how scientists may reject for a long time well-substantiated findings if these contradict established beliefs. Since the eighteenth century, when Volta challenged Galvani's assertion that frogs' legs operated electrically, most biologists have squelched or ignored evidence of animal electricity. The book chronicles in detail how clear findings presented by many others as well as Becker were repeatedly brushed off right up into the 1960s, when the scientific community finally began to accept that bodies generate electricity and are influenced by electromagnetic fields—a finding of far-reaching significance and practical value. In a postscript titled "Political Science," Becker exposes how the politics of funding determines the kind of research and therefore the kind of knowledge that is permitted.

Even today, prejudices against electrical healing, a heavy medical commitment to treatment by drugs or surgery, and commercial protection of microwave ovens and other electronically hazardous appliances still starve funding for research on electrical physiology. For questioning the safety to humans of various military and power installations radiating electromagnetism, Becker was deprived of all research funds and demoted from chief of research at a Veterans Adminstration hospital to night-admitting physician. Even today the United States government and the commercial companies it supposedly regulates will not admit an EM radiation hazard and resist research to investigate the possibility.

But besides these worldly factors, ever since Galvani's and Volta's day the mysterious and invisible power of electricity had been associated with the philosophy of vitalism, according to which the universe, as Plato and most other later philosophers taught, is animated from beyond itself by an immaterial force. Vitalists backed electricity as the candidate for this force while mechanists fought strenuously to disprove its presence in living beings, which electricity would appear to animate from another dimension. So a metaphysical dispute, potentially threatening the material basis of science itself, has underlain into our own time any research in bodily electricity. If researchers like Becker, well grounded in both medical practice and orthodox experimentation, have encountered such resistance in investigating purely physical phenomena, imagine the difficulty one may meet investigating less material phenomena.

Even Freud and Jung were intimidated by this conformist pressure, as Arthur Koestler points out in *The Roots of Consciousness:*

An Excursion into Parapsychology (1972). Though not personally inclined toward the paranormal, Freud came to believe in telepathy from direct experience of it with his patients and joined both the British and the American Society for Psychical Research. Ernest Jones dissuaded him from speaking or publishing about it, though Freud's papers on the relations between telepathy and psychoanalysis appeared posthumously. For most of his career, Jung felt obliged to explain his own numerous psychic experiences and his theory of the collective unconscious as somehow existing or happening in the individual mind, but near the end of his life he acknowledged that these had reality beyond the physical brain.

Though this sort of censorship has lifted somewhat today, physicist Fritjof Capra suffered career difficulties because he compared nuclear theory to oriental metaphysics in *The Tao of Physics* (1981). Biologist Rupert Sheldrake was castigated in an editorial titled "A Book for Burning?" (1981) in science's most prestigious and traditional journal, *Nature,* for the theory he set forth in *A New Science of Life: The Hypothesis of Formative Causation* (1981). Sheldrake hypothesizes that, along with heredity and environment, a nonmaterial field for each species may govern the formation of its members. It may be intellectually chic to speak of a "shift of paradigm" in the sciences, but it is not yet professionally very safe to propose one.

These examples are not idle. Not only is telepathy related to the idea of a collective unconscious or group mind like Sheldrake's formative field but both, if real, bear tremendously on learning. So let's use them further as examples of the bolder and broader research that educators might do well to foster and follow. Actually, the notion of intelligence as a force field exerting action across time and space has a tradition in modern biology that includes many others than Freud and Jung, who certainly took seriously the likelihood of such fields, since telepathy presupposes some such means of communication and since a collective unconscious would also depend on a nonphysical transmission in the present. ("Racial memory" begs the question of how individuals can remember experiences others had before them.)

Force Fields of Mind

One idea that recurs among scientists goes well beyond the now demonstrable fact that organisms give off an electromagnetic field.

It is that members of a set of living beings, including humans, participate in some kind of force field, escaping the detection of physical instruments, which individuals at once collectively generate and are in some measure directed by. Sheldrake calls these fields "morphogenetic" (from the traditional study of morphogenesis or developmental forces) to indicate that some characteristics of species are beamed to members in the present, beyond what genetic transmission can account for. Generally, according to this hypothesis, repeated action builds up a "morphic resonance" to which members are tuned and that perpetuates such action in the field until new actions have been repeated enough to change the field (as in evolution). The idea curiously resembles the Hindu *samskaras,* which are habits based on the self-perpetuating repetition of thoughts, words, and deeds that likewise generate a formative field by which the past determines the present. Experiments with people and animals before and after Sheldrake proposed his theory tend to indicate individuals may learn new behavior more easily after others have mastered it, a phenomenon that could explain the constant setting of new records in sports and of achievements in other fields that seem to extend human capacity. But certain proof for this controversial "new science of life" awaits, precisely, further research, which the *Brain/Mind Bulletin* faithfully covers, as it did the original controversy.

In the fall 1982 issue of *Revision,* Sheldrake placed his hypothesis within a lineage deriving from vitalists like Hans Driesch, an embryologist who defected from mechanism at the turn of the century because it could not explain how bits of an embryo could regenerate themselves, and from Alfred North Whitehead's organismic framework of the 1920s. Sheldrake's geneology of biologists proposing some sort of morphogenetic fields includes Alexander Gurwitsch of Russia, Paul Weiss of Vienna, C. H. Waddington, René Thom, and Brian Goodwin (p. 41). Writing before Sheldrake, in *The Roots of Coincidence* (1972), Koestler mentions that biologist Sir Alistair Hardy thought that the highly skilled and coordinated activities of some lower animals "could only be explained by a kind of group-mind where each individual shared a 'psychic blueprint' " (pp. 101–102).

In Lifetide: *The Biology of the Unconscious* (1979) another biologist, Lyall Watson, uses lifetide as a metaphor to evoke a field of interconnectedness among living things that may explain "paranormal" events such as the now famous "hundredth monkey" phenomenon. A young female monkey on a Japanese island began washing potatoes in the sea before eating them, a significant innovative behavior soon imitated by her peers and from them by their elders. Then on other Japanese islands other monkeys who could not have been learning from observation started washing their potatoes. Watson conjectures that after a certain critical mass has been reached—the hundredth monkey, say—the behavior becomes directly available to the whole collective unconscious of that group. This would of course exemplify exactly Sheldrake's idea, but, pertinently enough, Watson had to tell anecdotally the island-leaping part of the story because some researchers involved did not believe what was happening and those who did feared for their reputation if they reported it officially. Having to fill in this crucial gap in the journals with unofficial oral accounts brought Watson in for heavy criticism, especially from organizations that specialize in debunking quacks.

The common motive behind these various concepts of invisible formative fields has been to explain certain material observations that materialist frameworks cannot account for. Scientists who oppose a hypothesis like Sheldrake's tend to be biochemists, he points out, who work with a microview that obviates the inexplicable facts that zoologists and botanists encounter in the larger time-space scope of whole organisms and their evolution. Physicist David Bohm has proposed in *Wholeness and the Implicate Order* (1980) a theory comparable to Sheldrake's and for the similar reason that Bohm believes present-day quantum mechanics "does not have any concept of movement or process or continuity in time" because it too takes a microview (the momentaneous interactions of accelerated particles in a cloud chamber), "but out of this truncated view physicists are trying to explain everything" (Sheldrake and Bohm, 1982, p. 45). This from a highly respected former co-worker with Einstein and an author of a widely used textbook on quantum mechanics.

Like the morphogenetic field, Bohm's implicate order is a formative ground unmanifest itself but determining the particulars of what we do see. It is the enfolded, potential order behind the unfolded, manifest order and so corresponds, as Bohm does not hesitate to say, to metaphysical concepts of a nonphysical reality emanating the familiar material world. Sheldrake and Bohm agree on the similarity of their theories and of the theories' function, to make sense of the more comprehensive findings in their respective fields.

The limitations of physicalist assumptions have been forcefully impressed upon all the great brain researchers of the last hundred years. Michael Aron (1975) points out in the December 1975 issue of *Harper's* that I. V. Pavlov, Sir Charles Sherrington, Sir John Eccles, A. R. Luria, Wilder Penfield, and Karl Pribram all had to resort to positing some nonphysical plane or order of reality that, as in Sheldrake's and Bohm's theories, acts as a field governing what one observes. In *The Mystery of the Mind* (1975), after reporting his famous experiments with electrical stimulation of the brain, Wilder Penfield writes:

> Because it seems to me certain that it will always be quite impossible to explain the mind on the basis of neuronal action within the brain, and because it seems to me that the mind develops and matures independently throughout an individual's life as though it were a continuing element, and because a computer (which the brain is) must be programmed and operated by an agency capable of independent understanding, I am forced to choose the proposition that our being is to be explained on the basis of two fundamental elements. (p. 80)

Here Penfield is quite deliberately picking up a problem in the philosophy of science that was old in Newton's day—the one referred to earlier, about whether the universe is utterly mechanical or is animated by a force from another dimension. One of the "fundamental elements" would be physical and the other not. But like most other scientists today, Penfield hesitates to employ a term like "nonphysical" or "immaterial" because the definition of physical matter could simply be changed to fit the findings, as indeed may soon happen in a reconstrual of the nature of "nature" that can comfortably include the "supernatural."

Contrast Penfield's conclusion here, the same as his mentor Sherrington's and his other predecessors, with a statement in *The Dragons of Eden* (1977) by astronomist Carl Sagan, who was trying to head off just such a line of thinking in the public: "My fundamental premise about the brain is that its workings—what we sometimes call 'mind'—are a consequence of its anatomy and physiology, and nothing more" (p. 7 of the Introduction).

The current successor to the brain researcher's dilemma, Karl Pribram (1982), has brought theoretical physics and mathematics to bear on the brain/mind duality in such a way as to transcend the division into physical and nonphysical, natural and supernatural. He has adopted a holographic model based on the realization from Karl Lashley's and his own research that a memory has no particular brain site but is distributed over such a large portion of the brain that most removal or damage cannot destroy the memory. Just as each part of a hologram contains an image of the whole photographed object, different parts of the brain contain a record of a given experience.

Furthermore, in the same way that converging laser beams create a pattern of wave interference photographed as a hologram, although the pattern looks nothing like the photographed image, sensory wave frequencies intersecting at junctions between neurons register a pattern as a memory that also does not resemble the perceived object. "Images are mental constructions," Pribram writes in *The Holographic Paradigm.* "But the process of image construction involves . . . a transformation into the frequency (holographic) domain. This domain is characteristic not only of brain processing . . . but of physical reality as well. Bohm refers to it as the implicate order . . ." (1982 p. 33). Pribram continues, " . . . Time and space are collapsed in the frequency domain . . . . In the absence of space-time coordinates, the usual causality upon which scientific explanation depends must also be suspended" (p. 34). However much we might share Sagan's concern that knowledge not be polluted by popular superstition, educators must recognize that the scientific paradigm is rapidly shifting among leading researchers to accommodate formally what Sir Arthur Eddington said for some scientists even several decades ago, that the stuff of the universe is mind-stuff.

A hypothesis should not be ruled out of serious consideration because it is physically untestable. After all, the more comprehensive and important an idea, the harder we should expect it to be to confirm empirically. If we insist on material evidence, we doom our understanding of nature to the less consequential. Rather, we may avail ourselves of other ways of testing an hypothesis. First, how well does it explain otherwise inexplicable phenomena? Second, how well generally does it fit knowledge already accepted? Third, though no experiment may be devised to test it directly, does a synthesis of empirical evidence culled over time from across different disciplines tend to bear it out? Finally, are there logical ways to reason a case for it? Research that truly contributes to education in the future will have to help us understand better the relations among thought, language, and consciousness. This will not happen without considering seriously some ideas not so honored so far in education, though given considerable thought on the growing edge of the scientific community.

Entertaining the idea, for example, of mental force fields acting in exemption from time and space would make an enormous difference in how we might think about language learning. If collective consciousness and telepathy are real, what new truths might these imply, and what light would they shed on old facts? Koestler says that Freud "theorised that ESP was an archaic method of communication between individuals, which was later supplanted by the more efficient method of sensory communication" (1972). If this is true, we *must* know it, because the ramifications are enormous. Reflect a moment on the import of such an idea for language acquisition and for the roles of speech and literacy, especially to the extent childhood may recapitulate history. Does language, for example, supplant telepathy for the child, as Freud theorized it once did for humanity as a whole? If so, in what sense does the child gain? Are there losses? What effect does the acquisition of speech have on cognition and consciousness? There may be no more important question for learning. It is not nearly enough to assume that language is all good and to focus only on how to further its acquisition.

And if morphogenetic fields exist, a human individual must be participating in several at once—familial, ethnic, linguistic, cultural. How do these interplay? Of the several fields to which an individual is tuned which field dominates in influence? Dominates by virtue of which factors? What is the relation between knowledge beamed directly and constantly to the individual from these group minds and knowledge learned by personal experience or by oral and written transmission? Are people in fact gaining access telepathically to knowledge that is attributed to deliberate teaching? What opens or blocks attunement to these fields (and some perhaps beyond the human families)? Can people learn to control attunement so as to choose which field to resonate with at a certain moment?

Let's begin to move this inquiry closer to language learning by using as transition a couple of lines of valuable research already in progress. One was begun some thirty years ago by H. A. Witkin, who proposed a psychological dimension running from field-dependent to field-independent where 'field' refers to a physical or social environment. Originated in investigations of how much people orient themselves spatially by internal versus external references, this initially perceptual dimension has since become a common dimension of cognitive style and of personality and has even been usefully applied to cultural comparison, as in the finding that individuals in hunter-gatherer societies tend toward independence from the social field whereas members of herder-farmer societies tend to depend more on the group. These differences are reflected in their respective ways of rearing children. Because language is social in origin and in function, the degree of individual dependence on the group must affect considerably how one learns and practices language, especially as this degree itself is in part culturally determined. But this whole promising line of investigation of one's relations to the social field might take a quantum leap if researchers saw fit to consider research subjects within several sorts of fields, perhaps simultaneously sometimes, one possibility being physically detectable fields such as those of gravity and electromagnetism, another being the more inferential fields of society and culture, and another being the "immaterial" fields of collective telepathic knowledge.

With a more enabling concept of "field," research might yield greater understanding about familiar practical learning issues. Does truly mastering a foreign language, for example, entail participation in a new group mind, a new attunement? Do small children learn a native language so rapidly and foreign languages so much more readily than elders because they are more telepathically receptive? Does our current concept of literacy, that the learner joins a community of readers and writers, mean more than we know, in the sense that joining is not just learning by interacting with people physically present but tapping into the whole pool of the literate group mind of one's society? How different is a literate field from an oral field? Putting the question anew like this might help us make better use of what a Walter Ong or an Eric Havelock tells us about the relations of orality to literacy.

The most neglected problem in education may be why children go into a slump by the end of primary school, around the age of eight. As psychologist Joseph Chilton Pearce described probably most forcefully, in *The Magical Child* (1977), a prodigious creative learning capacity enjoyed during the preschool and primary years seems to wither then. Do language acquisition and external acculturation cause this as a side effect by overmolding experience? This paramount question might become more answerable if researchers were willing to recast it into terms of group-mind resonance. Does orality first, and then literacy again later, alter the receptivity of the individual to such resonance—reduce telepathy and hence make it harder to gain direct access to the pool of collective knowledge? Does shifting cultural transmission from telepathy to oral and written language free individuals from the tyranny of an unconscious group mind only to cut them off from the genius of the genus, with all its accumulated knowledge and capacity, and set them plodding to piece this all together bit by bit? Researchers are going around and around, as in the debate between the followers of Chomsky and Piaget, about how much environment and heredity, nurture and nature, contribute respectively to human formation. This forum may need another dimension—the ways in which morphogenetic fields are forming the mind directly, interplaying with these physical and social fields.

The Evolution of Consciousness

The work of psychologist Julian Jaynes exemplifies both some directions for new research and some limitations of the old. In *The Origin of Consciousness in the Breakdown of the Bicameral Mind,* (1976) he sets forth a daring thesis based on an admirable synthesis of knowledge from art and archaeology, physiology and psychiatry, myth and history. Before about three thousand years ago, he argues, individuals did not experience personal consciousness and could not think for themselves. They depended almost totally on the culture and had a "bicameral mind," by which he means a two-chambered mind of which half carried out orders received from the other half, which was really a program of cultural imperatives perceived by the individual as voices of gods or ancestors. Jaynes hypothesizes as the mechanism for this bicamerality that these standing orders were transmitted from an area in the right hemisphere of the brain to a corresponding area in the left hemisphere (Wernicke's area, a major site of speech), where they were translated into hallucinated voices. So people felt directly commanded to act by the gods, as in the *Iliad,* and were indeed run from the outside.

Two developments broke down the bicameral mind, says Jaynes, and made today's personal consciousness develop as a necessity.

Mobility confused the cultures, and literacy silenced the voices. When cultures began to mix, individual action was confounded beyond the capacity of programmed commands. At the same time, laws inscribed to be posted or circulated replaced the hallucinated vocal directives. (Moses' bringing down of the tablets would presumably represent a transition.) Individual mentation became necessary for action, and literacy made it possible by teaching people to metaphorize and hence to build an inner model of the world. So consciousness evolves from group to individual but with many throwbacks to remote authority as in the auditory hallucinations of modern schizophrenics.

In its ingenious weaving of disparate information and its application in turn to different domains, the theory is brilliant if only one-quarter true, because even what may not be true catalyzes very productive thinking in the reader. Here are some thoughts from this reader. First, some notion of evolution in consciousness does seem prerequisite for discussing in depth the other matters of language acquisition, cognitive development, and cultural heritage. Second, such a comprehensive framework does entail a rare sort of scanning across areas of knowledge and across periods of history. It was heroic to attempt this alone. Third, the direction of the evolution of consciousness that Jaynes indicates, from collective to individual, seems well confirmed by many other things he does not refer to, as does also his splendid evocation of the waning of the gods and the fading of the voices, so well attested in a vast mythology and literature of lost paradises and in the long subsequent history of efforts to reestablish contact through divination, auguries, prophecies, and other seership by those still gifted to hear divine or ancestral voices. (Yeats: "The falcon can no longer hear the falconer.") Finally, and this does not exhaust the riches of the theory, Jaynes illuminates past and present by bringing them to bear on each other in a living continuity pertinent to the purposes of education.

The drawbacks of Jaynes's thesis reflect the limitations of his profession and his culture. Let's begin with his date for the origin of our sort of consciousness. It's set too late. His timetable of causation obliged him to place it after the advent of writing, but in writings as early as the *Vedas,* which are surely transcriptions of long oral traditions, meditation practices are referred to as antedating writing and presuppose a personal consciousness already so developed that it needed to be quieted and reattuned to fields beyond. The metaphorization that Jaynes sees as inaugurating individual consciousness more likely *prepared* for writing than *resulted* from it. That is, it seems easier to imagine metaphorization deriving from visual homologues such as tree limbs/body limbs, from which in turn could develop the categorical concepts needed for common nouns and further verbalization.

Here I feel Jaynes is following our common cultural assumption that thought is beholden to language. Our culture bears nearly as strong a bias against the nonverbal as it does against the nonphysical. Language is revered out of all measure, at least by those who make their living by it, to the point that we can hardly imagine the mind developing without it, whereas as Hans Furth, for one, has pointed out in *Thinking Without Language: Psychological Implications of Deafness* (1966), thought can grow independently of language. But the very perceptiveness of the rest of Jaynes's theory calls our attention to this telling assumption that, precisely, needs much more thought and research. It is most likely that vocalization became speech in the measure that thinking was already developing and pressing for a means of communicating itself, though, once associated, each fostered the other.

More important, the materialist framework of the scientific establishment within which Jaynes is still trying to work obliges him to contain the voices within the physical brain, as hallucination, whereas I think the bicameral or externally directed mind can be better explained by telepathy and better developed by the concept of a collective mental force field operating from the past and within the present. This adjustment would not seriously disrupt Jaynes's thesis, but it would alter the relations among thought, speech, writing, and consciousness—which are all the more important for educators as children may pass through whatever sequence humanity may have undergone. So, according to my own theorizing, thought evolved before speech—conceptualization independently of verbalization—but was group thought, shared by telepathy, which can be wordless. What we call "instinct" in animals, which permits them to do astonishing things that they never learned, may be just this nonverbal collective consciousness operating across a whole species.

The mixing of bloods and cultures did indeed muddy each group mind, however, and did force individuals to think for themselves. The emergence of individual consciousness, speech, and literacy are indeed related to each other and to the disappearance of the gods and voices, but it could as easily have happened as follows. If speech evolved out of the necessity to replace telepathy, it was because the development of personal consciousness was already weakening the attunement with the collective consciousness.

Consciousness would be evolving, as Jaynes and others indicate, from group to individual. Effect rather than cause of this evolution, literacy would nevertheless have made personal consciousness at once more necessary and more possible as it replaced telepathy. Hallucination probably did occur as a frantic effort to renew contact with the authoritarian imperatives. Being in touch with the culture externally but out of touch with the group mind internally could have left us with the nostalgia for ethnocentricity that today plagues not only world peace but haunts cultural research itself. Understanding the direction of the evolution of consciousness deserves top priority, because educators need to think about how schooling should fit this development.

Another cultural bias may play a part in Jaynes's theory that is critical to thinking about the evolution of consciousness, namely, the notion that our age is superior to the past. Thus he posits a pathological behavior like hallucination to explain how our former mind was externally directed, not a positive faculty like telepathy, which modern people usually don't have access to or don't believe in but would envy in earlier people were they indeed endowed with it. (The esoteric literature, which we will soon examine, consistently assumes telepathic consciousness and the evolution of this into personal consciousness.)

A notion of progress that condescends to the past destroys the very concept of evolution in consciousness, which must acknowledge that trade-offs occur over history among human faculties. Memory and reason, let's say for example, became respectively necessary to create and retain knowledge as human beings became more individuated and lost telepathic touch with the group field. Misleading value judgments can enter here. Moderns are more willing to concede that preliterate peoples had a better memory, because we regard memory as an inferior faculty, whereas telepathy, if accepted, would appear to be "higher." But if consciousness is evolving from collective to individual, then of course telepathy would be most appropriate to the earlier, collective stage. And also, the evolution of consciousness may well spiral so that, for example, telepathy might return as a willed capacity that individuals might switch on and off rather than, as previously, an unconscious, involuntary bond to which no alternative for knowledge existed before memory and reason. Thus, just as personal memory of acquired experience would have taken the place of the waning telepathic group mind, so memory would have had to decline before logic could fully flourish.

If literacy triggers intellectual growth, it may be because it undercuts memory and makes reason needed as a supplanting means to knowledge. If you can't tune it in or recall it, figure it out. Maybe we should regard reason as both a third-best and a cumulative achievement. So it is in this evolutionary way that we must consider the interplay of faculties, and not mourn this loss or vaunt that gain. It may come about that as the technology of printing made memory less necessary but brought reason to the fore, the technology of computers may cause logic to atrophy and force a yet more sophisticated knowledge-making faculty to emerge.

Cultural Literacy as Cross-Cultural Fluency

Still, isn't all this too speculative, unprovable? How can research be research and depart so far from the evidence of the senses? Part of the point is that research has always been more speculative than it appears. And the more "proof" accumulates the more it topples of its own weight. Hence the "deconstruction" occurring now in philosophy: greater knowledge has led to greater uncertainty about the larger, more important matters. Research needs to become more frankly speculative, philosophical, and even metaphysical, because such frameworks cannot truly be omitted, they can only be secreted or disregarded.

Partialities are not just personal and partisan but cultural. In fact it is from the cultural that we discover how much we still function as a group mind. Ethnocentricity, more than anything else, limits understanding. Personal and partisan biases can detect and counter each other, and a synthesis of disciplines can offset the limitations of each field of formal investigation, but what is to correct cultural partialities? Yes, other cultures, at least to a great degree, but research rarely crosses cultures. The corrective is to draw not only on other current cultures but on those of the past, for impartiality–the *whole* truth—requires tension over time as well as space.

To focus these considerations and relate them more to the classroom, let's cast them into the terms of the "cultural literacy" debate, which concerns whether schools should identify and teach to everyone certain key ideas, values, and works deemed to characterize the culture in which the education is to occur. Immediately one wonders how a culture is defined for this purpose. Most states have required their students to take courses in the history and culture of their state or region, and most U.S. schools have required courses in American history and American literature, often leaving ancient or European history, or British or European literature, as options, though sometimes the course in the larger culture may be required as well.

Advocates of Great Books have in mind a coverage or sampling of "Western" culture, alleged to have begun with the Greeks but allowing that Christianity had roots in Judaism. To designate those classics that culturally literate students ought to have read, educators often refer to them, by analogy with holy writ, as the "canon" (other books being presumably apocryphal). Of course actually "covering" a culture so defined necessitates students' reading a great deal in translation and instructors' surveying for students a vast amount that their charges could not be expected to read for themselves. So besides the partialities built into the culture itself, we must take into account the endless possibilities for misrepresentation that inhere in all this purveying of three millenia of culture, at each stage of which the inheritors are selecting, translating, and summarizing according to their bents and lights. Characterizing a culture poses a profoundly compounded problem in research, inasmuch as each generation of researchers is somewhat at the mercy of all its predecessors as well as of its own predilections.

Recent efforts to make "cultural literacy" a central curriculum goal may well owe much to the threat posed to national and cultural identity during the last twenty years by the self-assertion of old minorities like blacks and Hispanics and by new immigrations of Southeast Asians, Central and South Americans, West Indians, and Middle-Easterners. But the threat to identity comes from without as well as from within. Commerce, finance, politics, and ecological safety are rapidly becoming internationalized. The interdependence among countries is creating so sensitive and intricate a fabric that the very viability and validity of nations is coming into question, and the need for planetary regulation and cooperation is coming to the fore, pioneered by the European Community. At the same time, the United States has been losing the supreme position it enjoyed following World War II and is becoming just another nation striving to hold its own in international competition. Backlashes of nationalism and ethnocentricity have resulted from all this, including the gratifications of Desert Storm.

When in 1988 Stanford changed its required course in Western civilization to include non-European cultures and works by women and members of minorities, U.S. Education Secretary William Bennett charged that this was "primarily a political, not an educational decision" and that ethnicity had nothing to do with it (Bennett, 1988). But the very definition of a culture is political, and nothing has so much to do with a culture as ethnicity. This inability or unwillingness to acknowledge these substrata of books and ideas is something the future will not abide.

Research can play a perhaps salvational role in dealing with the conflicts inherent in the educational goal of cultural literacy. As Europeans and Americans have had increasingly to share scholarly authority with researchers of other cultures, a less parochial perspective of civilization has emerged. In his trilogy *Black Athena: The Afroasiatic Roots of Classical Civilization* (1987), historian Martin Bernal argues on considerable evidence that the Greek language and culture derived from Egypt and Phoenicia, as stated by the Greeks themselves, but that European scholars of the eighteenth and nineteenth centuries, mostly British and German, discredited these derivations from Africa and the Orient for ethnocentric and racist reasons, establishing instead an "Aryan Model" that kept the founts of "Western" civilization in Europe and hence its great works in the family. Bernal's ongoing trilogy has ignited an ongoing controversy over his thesis, first given a forum in a special issue of *Arethusa* in the fall of 1989 and now aired even in the popular press. Bernal traces in great detail how European scholarly vogues for Rome, Egypt, China, India, and Greece succeeded themselves during the last two centuries until preference settled on Greece, around which many great scholars of the period constructed a godlike mystique befitting Caucasian and Christian superiority. This Hellenophilia influences powerfully today even an eminent classicist like Eric Havelock. When he claims in *The Muse Learns to Write* (1986) that the Greeks invented the first real alphabet and thereby became the first philosophers, he combines this cultural assumption of Greek primacy with the cultural assumption that intellectual achievement awaits literacy.

It is true, as one can see for oneself, that many if not most of the great scholars of the last century, on whose work we often rely, were startlingly chauvinistic. In the Introduction to his 1882 translation of the Chinese classic *The I Ching: Book of Changes,* James Legge's irritation with his subject erupts more than once. He makes invidious comparisons with Western texts, calls the hexagrams themselves a "farrago" (p. 25), and disparages the philosophy when it doesn't resemble Christian doctrine. This was the standard translation until Richard Wilhelm's in 1950, published by Princeton's Bollingen Foundation and introduced by Jung.

But consider a far more recent work, also much relied on, Montague Rhodes James' *The Apocryphal New Testament,* put out in 1924 by Oxford University. In his preface James cheerfully explains that a main reason for making the texts available is to show how they deserved to be excluded from the Bible. He then gives as reasons for his excluding Gnostic texts even from his Apocrypha that Gnostics were not "normal or Catholic Christians" (p. xvii); that the texts, which he named, were unavailable (though he deemed it his job to translate and make scores of other texts available); and that they were not readable or made little sense. Thus this twentieth century scholar carried on the censorship of the Gnostic literature that Irenaeus and other church fathers had initiated so successfully in the second century that Gnostics rarely spoke for themselves until the accidental discovery in 1945 of the Gnostic Gospels at Nag Hammadi in Upper Egypt, buried there in the fourth century to escape Roman Christian scourging.

In *The Sufis* and other works, scholar Idries Shah has pointed out how much more some sources of Western literature and other culture lie in Arabic civilization than most Americans and Europeans realize. He refers not just to known works such as *A Thousand and One Nights,* which provided the concept of a frame story for a collection of stories, borrowed by Boccaccio for *The Decameron* and from Boccaccio by Chaucer for *The Canterbury Tales,* and traced by its most popular translator Sir Richard Francis Burton back to Indian "parrot stories," in which a series of stories is told within the frame of a larger story. Nor does he refer merely to the Sufi allegory "The Rubaiyat of Omar Khayam"—which Edward Fitzgerald fashioned into a classic of wine, women, and song—but also to the troubadour and Grail literature of the twelfth and thirteenth centuries, medieval scholasticism, and the work of such figures as Dante, Roger Bacon, and St. John of the Cross. Europeans have never fully acknowledged how much "Western" culture has drawn from, interacted with, or at least been preserved and transmitted by this "other" culture.

Ever since studying Chaucer in college I wondered about the origin of the tradition from which he got the strange idea of his *Parliament of Fowls.* Years later my wife came across a copy of *The Conference of the Birds,* a twelfth-century Sufi allegory by Farid Ud-din Attar. In the full-year course in Chaucer that I took at Harvard in 1952 no such Eastern tradition was mentioned. In the scholarly edition read in the course, F. N. Robinson's *The Poems of Chaucer* (1933) in the Cambridge Poets series of Houghton Mifflin, we are simply told that the device, "familiar in medieval literature, of a council or parliament of birds . . . has no definite source or model, but draws freely for its materials from French, Latin, and Italian" (p. 361). Could American scholars not have known of a work four times translated into English (including by the renowned Burton, who considered it a key text) and so well regarded in Islam that a new edition of it has appeared every few years since the twelfth century in one or another country of the Near East? If not known, why not? And if known, why not mentioned?

It is difficult to distinguish cultural chauvinism from religious competition. Christian censorship over the centuries deliberately removed knowledge of other religious and cultural influences such as Manicheism, which was Persian, and Gnosticism, which flourished in Egypt and the Levant. The showdown during the first centuries after Christ between Rome and Alexandria, which Rome of course won, typify the West's periodic efforts to purge itself of the East. The chief reason for the Christian burning of libraries at Alexandria (the Saracens also burned some later) and for the murder there by monks of Hypatia, the brilliant, renowned female mathematician/philosopher, was to destroy that great Afroasiatic pagan culture, which succeeded that of Athens and surpassed that of Rome. Bernal's point that European civilization was never limited to the northern shores of the Mediterranean—to Europe—involves controversies about which cultures were antecedent and which derivative. Many Christian scholars have tried to prove, for example, that both Egyptian and Greek religions derived from the teachings of Moses.

But an equally important point, typified by Alexandria, concerns the constant synthesis of cultures occurring not only in the ancient world but all through history. Ideas have been so syncretized, inventions and discoveries so cycled around cultures and built on from one to another, that it becomes ludicrous to start assigning credit, especially to one's "own." When Aristotle's pupil Alexander founded his Greek city in Egypt, he was bringing back to the "East" in a new form ideas that came from there, and his Hellenism then became utterly fused with cultures stretching from Iran to India that were, like Egypt, now receiving back through his conquests a transformation of what they had earlier contributed to.

What Alexandria was to the ancient world, the Languedoc area of southern France was to the medieval world—a rich fusion of cultures that the Christian empire destroyed because it was offering a whole alternative civilization. Up over the Pyrenees in the eleventh to thirteenth centuries there spilled an astonishing hybrid culture that was part Christian, part Jewish, and part Islamic, but harmonious. From it was generated not only part of the troubadour Grail literature but the Albigensian or Cathar heresy and the Knights Templar, both of which the church and the government of France ruthlessly exterminated. Jewish Cabalism, Muslim Sufism, and Christian mysticism not only coexisted for a while in Spain and southern France but enriched each other and produced an illuministic strain of culture that, had it been allowed to survive, could have vastly improved "Western civilization" and that in any case was to prolong subterraneanly into modern times the multicultural esoteric doctrine of antiquity.

And here we come upon some little discussed matters that future research should certainly bring out into the open and deal with if cultural literacy is to be more than a kind of academically glamorized jingoism. Beneath cultures that we think of as different there seems to run a universal substrate, but this does not come through in traditional history partly because history is usually written ethnocentrically from within one culture (or even a faction of a culture) and partly because what is common to different cultures is a universalist metaphysic transmitted more or less secretly and quite often in oral forms that escape most historians. (See Rudolf Steiner's *Occult History* [1957] as an antidote.) Because it is about the cosmic, this underground culture is cosmopolitan—international, cross-cultural, and remarkably consistent over time despite its many transformations.

A Universal Metaphysic

Moot and buried as it is, this sort of metaphysical common denominator may deserve highest priority in future research, for several reasons. Substantiating it could show that (1) all cultures are at bottom kin and can identify with each other; (2) minorities belong to whatever culture they're in because whatever other culture they originated from has contributed to the one they're now in, as African, Asiatic, and Semitic have to "Western"; (3) to become culturally literate about one culture has to mean about all cultures, simultaneously—about culture and acculturation; and (4) this universal metaphysic may provide just the sort of comprehensive framework for future investigation that will benefit not only educational subjects like literacy and literature but knowledge generally.

My own studies for many years have focused on what is variously called the "perennial philosophy" (the title of Aldous Huxley's [1944] work on the subject, taken from Leibnitz), the "wisdom literature," the "esoteric doctrine," and so forth. This is the universal metaphysic, just mentioned, that has been transmitted across cultures from preliterate times to the present, taught in the ancient world through various "mysteries" and in the Middle Ages through Christian heresies and such channels as the Knights Templar and the Cabalists. It posits a cosmology of multiple realities successively precipitating from rarer to denser—metaphorically speaking!—and correspondingly informing people as multiple levels of being. It surfaced during the Renaissance as Rosicrucianism (Spenser's Red Cross Knight reflects it) and in the eighteenth century as Freemasonry, the form of it that so profoundly influenced the Enlightenment and the men who founded the United States. Today it is represented by the Theosophists, Rudolf Steiner's Anthroposophy, some Rosicrucians, and various New Age groups. Steiner's many books build up a stunning presentation of its thought, history, and applications to the twentieth century. Max Heindel's *The Roscicrucian Cosmo-Conception* (1909) treats it most fully in a single text. But the book that best covers it across its various traditions, and does so through copious quotations and old illustrations, is Manley Hall's *The Secret Teachings of All Ages* (1978).

At times the teaching took on the transformative language of alchemy or the force-field language of astrology, both of which, like official church teachings themselves, were frequently debased by people unready to understand their symbols. Indeed, the danger of misunderstanding and consequent abuse was the chief reason this doctrine was kept esoteric, secret—a later reason being also to escape persecution. People today perhaps more even than then are almost bound to misunderstand the language and imagery of these traditions, because we read the symbols too materially and read into them the "prescientific" ignorance and superstition we expect to find and which indeed abounded all about this subtle metaphysic, often as popular degenerations of it. Jung, however, spent the last seventeen years of his life studying alchemy, because he knew better, and because he knew the esoteric tradition perhaps better than any other investigator of our time not actually transmitting the teaching like Steiner, Heindel, Helena Blavatsky, and Alice Bailey.

Most of the "West's" great philosophers were participating, more or less awarely, in this tradition, as Liebnitz acknowledged in his term *philosophia perennia.* The esoteric literature takes for granted part of what Martin Bernal is documenting in *Black Athena* (1987), that Pythagoras, Plato, and the other Greek philosophers were—themselves, not just the Neoplatonists!—all working off of Egyptian Hermeticism. But the latter itself is regarded by esotericists as incorporating elements from Mesopotamia and India and having antecedents as well in whatever the civilization of Atlantis was. We may find it hard to believe that preliterate cultures could have had thoughts deep and subtle enough to have been worthy of transmission and transformation by the finest minds of "our" civilization. Indeed, we tend to date a culture from its first texts—Homer and the Bible—as if these were not vestiges of oral and nonverbal traditions predating writing by many centuries.

Most scholars still argue, for example, that the Hermetic texts can't represent an expression of Egyptian thought because they were written in Latin and Greek circa the first couple of centuries after Christ and clearly contain Platonic and Stoic ideas! In the only version most English-language readers are likely to find of these texts—another publication by Oxford in 1924, *Hermetica*—editor-translator Walter Scott first rules half of the corpus out of his collection on grounds that they are "pseudoscience" and "rubbish" not connected to the religious philosophy of the other half (p. 4 of the Introduction). He then proceeds to speculate that these anonymous authors ascribed their texts to Hermes (Egyptian Thoth, scribe of the gods and inventor of writing) only because "it had long been accepted as a known historical fact that both Pythagoras and Plato had studied in Egypt" and so their writings would gain prestige from associating them with this illustrious genealogy. Of the original Egyptian writings themselves, such as *The Book of the Dead,* this authority writes on the same page that "it may seem strange to us that anyone should have imagined them to contain a profound philosophy." Though Scott believes that these writers were merely recasting Greek thought for themselves, he acknowledges that they themselves "were teaching what they held to be the supreme and essential truth towards which Greek philosophy pointed; and it was taken as known that Greek philosophy was derived from the Egyptian books of Hermes, in which that essential truth was taught" (p. 5 of the Introduction).

The very founders of modern science—Newton, Bacon, and Descartes—were so steeped in the esoteric doctrine that half of what they said has been passed over in embarrassment by those moderns who don't realize that physics cannot be disembedded from metaphysics. When Descartes said that the seat of the soul is in the pineal gland, he was merely passing on an idea transmitted to him from the esoteric doctrine and found in the Vedanta as well as in the Hermetica (and made less embarrassing perhaps by recent research on the pineal, regarded until the last few decades as vestigial, like the appendix, but now likely to replace the pituitary as the "master gland"). For the same reason, however, that some Christians don't want to admit influences from pagan and heretical sources, some members of the scientific community don't want to acknowledge how much the fathers of modern science were inspired by their background in the esoteric doctrine, which includes of course the now anathematized alchemy and astrology.

In one of periodic efforts to stave off such an unholy relationship, a conference was held at U.C.L.A. in 1974 to counter the credence that some of the scientific community was showing in such theses as historian Francis Yates's, that Giordano Bruno and other esotericists of his time adopted the Copernican theory because it corresponded to their Hermetic metaphysic. One of the papers delivered there, published in *Hermeticism and the Scientific Revolution* (Westman and McGuire, 1977), was by a Newton specialist, J. E. McGuire, who says, "Although Newton's alchemical manuscripts lend support to the position that the general character of his pre-1680 views on the aether and the powers of light may derive from alchemical texts, this claim should be treated with caution" inasmuch as, he continues weakly, we don't know from his reading notes on them or from his commentary on them what he thought of them (p. 119). Despite this ignorance, McGuire goes on to say that "no matter how it is interpreted, alchemy cannot explain the genesis and nature of Newton's claim that light and bodies are 'convertible into one another' " because *McGuire* sees nothing compatible to this idea in alchemy, although in the same breath he says that "Newton probably saw alchemy as a deep and esoteric expression of true knowledge that had to be properly interpreted . . . ." (p. 120). Indeed, the idea of conversion between light and bodies is more than compatible with the esoteric cosmology of successive emanations, rarer to denser, eventually manifesting the world we know. Here in this cosmology, by the way, is surely a precursor, via Newton, of the concept that energy and matter are convertible into one another, formulated as $E = mc^2$ by Einstein, who was not at all embarrassed by metaphysics, of whomever's culture.

In *The New View Over Atlantis* archaeologist John Michell wrote, in regard to the worldwide megalithic culture of monuments, mounds, and alignments, that we live amid the fragments of a vast human creation we do not see the whole of or the purpose of. This is exactly how I have come to feel about the esoteric doctrine, which may be central to our ultimate understanding of knowledge and learning. We know bits of it from literature, religion, history, and philosophy, but scholars have never put it together so as either to interpret the pieces properly or to discern its coherence and continuity through "Western" and other cultures. For research it poses the inherent problems of having been transmitted secretly, often orally, or nonverbally through glyphs, so that it does not always manifest in texts, and when it does, the texts may be regarded as about something else, or as unintelligible, like Plato's *Timaeus,* his most esoteric and probably least read work today.

Indeed, I suspect that many important texts have been ill translated by scholars not conversant enough with esoteric tradition to understand fully the content of the texts, like even the great translator of the Egyptian *The Book of the Dead,* Wallace Budge (1895), who could have better rendered the intricate Egyptian spectrum of realities had he better known its counterpart in esoteric Christian, Jewish, and Islamic teachings. This might in turn have helped Walter Scott to translate and edit the *Hermetica.* But, paradoxically, the very ubiquity of the esoteric doctrine makes it accessible if researchers know to look for it and enjoy a spacious enough purview to be able to connect its scattered and various manifestations.

The more serious problem is that modern academics and intellectuals have been little inclined to pursue it for fear of being associated with superstition or "occultism," which has sensationalist connotations in America, where also the scientific inquisition has reigned most punitively. Ironically, the scientific establishment inherited this taboo from the religious establishment, which profoundly resented a teaching more spiritual than its own exoteric popularizations of it and that was, furthermore, transmitted outside the church.

Thus both establishments have kept from public awareness and from standard American history books, as noted earlier, the fact that international Freemasonry played a decisive role in establishing modern democracy. The old Jesuitical conspiracy theory originated by Abbé de Barruel in 1797, still much alive today in extreme right circles, correctly traces Freemasonry back through the esoteric chain to Egyptian Hermeticism but makes of it a satanic force bent on destroying Christian civilization. For example, *Secret Societies and Subversive Movements* (Webster, 1924), a scholarly book by a British lady of the twenties, currently published in America by the Christian Book Club of America and distributed by the John Birch Society, opens with this sentence: "The East is the cradle of secret societies." The lineage she reconstructs matches remarkably the one that esotericists trace for themselves, only she is unearthing it in order to warn the world of its conspiracy.

In *The Mythology of the Secret Societies* (1972), J. M. Roberts argues that the Masons could not as an organization have plotted the French Revolution, which actually decimated its ranks. Charles Heckethorn's seminal two-volume work of 1885 and 1897, *The Secret Societies of All Ages and Countries,* presented the esoteric tradition as a regenerative force in civilization. To judge from his novel *Foucault's Pendulum* (1988), Italian scholar Umberto Eco has accumulated enormous erudition about this tradition but is less interested in what it is about than in what jaded postmoderns have spawned about it by way of satirizable conspiracy theories and faddist cults in Europe, where, we note, the tradition is far better known than in America. In *Gnosis: A Journal of the Western Traditions* (winter, 1990) reviewers Deborah Belle Forman and Jay Kinney, (also the journal's editor) interpreted Eco's novel as disparagement of the tradition if not a downright return, under all the academic and literary sophistication, to Catholic denunciation of an ancient enemy. At any rate, advocates of right-wing conspiracy theorists like Catholic Nesta Webster share with many academic people of the twentieth century a revulsion to the esoteric doctrine and a repudiation of the "East" that engendered it.

Modern scholars can best avoid rebukes from both scientific and religious quarters if they just ignore the whole matter of the role in overt events of this underground strand of civilization, even though this strand most likely constitutes the single most important continuity in it, if not the very substrate of it. This buried but all-pervasive cosmology must be declassified, nevertheless, history deconstructed, and culture reconstructed on pain of much interim research merely compounding the problems and their attendant distortions. That is, the partialities we have inherited in default of the total, universalist teaching have skewed our view of knowledge and rendered much research useless or misleading.

Lit Crit and Holy Writ

My own studies in the esoteric traditions have greatly impressed on me how much more profoundly they have influenced literature than traditional studies indicate, as in the case of Chaucer's *The Parliament of Fowls,* where not only may the author be unaware of all that is in the stories or symbols he is taking over but where equally culture-bound scholars may not know either. Of course literary scholars already know a lot about neoplatonism or the terms and tropes of a tradition like alchemy if only to be able to gloss the allusions to them in medieval or Renaissance texts. But the full relation between literature and the esoteric teachings has hardly begun to emerge. Most American literature professors who know of *The Occult Philosophy in the Elizabethan Age* (1979), by the much honored late British historian Dame Francis Yates, don't take her work seriously though George Steiner and other scholars abroad praised it, probably because she was pioneering in precisely the threat-laden direction just indicated. She relates key works like *The Faerie Queen, The Alchemist,* Marlowe's *Faust,* and *The Tempest* to Christian cabalists such as Raymond Lull, Pico della Mirandola, Cornelius Agrippa, and the much caricatured John Dee, resident magus of Elizabeth's court. (Shakespeare and Spenser seem to have honored the esoteric tradition while Jonson and Marlowe seem to have distrusted it, but this needs more study.) We have only to look at the work of the Romantics, the French Symbolists, Yeats, Eliot, Joyce, and Pound to realize how intimately this tradition has remained a part of literature.

But the most far-reaching aspect of the relationship concerns less the conscious participation of authors in the tradition as the subtle workings of it on the most profane writers. In fact, I would like to see researchers take on the hypothesis that all literature in any culture is a secularization of some holy writ that is in turn a localized version of a universal metaphysic. The earliest literature is sacred and cosmological, the following literature does a kind of exegesis on this scripture, the next a commentary on the exegesis in turn (*Torah, Talmud, Midrashim*), and so on and on through retelling and reinterpreting, the sources becoming outwardly dimmer as they become more incorporated.

The religious but worldly Chaucer seems unaware that his story of a courtly love contest among the fowls on St. Valentine's Day (*The Parliament of Fowls*) secularizes an allegory of pilgrims seeking self-realization in the Great Spirit, explicitly expressed in the Sufi text (*The Conference of Birds*) through what the birds discuss and through the story itself of traveling to a great figure who is themselves and into whom they merge. Cicero's "Dream of Scipio," furthermore, which Chaucer exploits to introduce his dream vision, so popular in medieval times, was one of the great esoteric texts of antiquity, a classic literary account of a spirit-guided journey to other realms, with which esoteric literature is saturated, modeled on the out-of-body mystery initiations that the hierophants provided around the Mediterranean for centuries before the advent of Christ (who entranced Lazarus for this same purpose and opened up the heavens for Peter, James, and John during the Transfiguration).

As Chaucer imagined himself guided to another world, like Cicero, by Scipio Africanus, Dante had imagined himself guided through Hell and Paradise by Vergil and Beatrice, and Vergil had had himself guided into Hell by the Sybil. Vergil had only to draw from the mysteries going on all around him, which at some point secularized themselves into some sort of awesome spectacle *symbolizing* such a trance journey or astral travel. This may be the point at which literature took over from the actual transformative ordeal of these initiations, rendered in myths of being stolen off, like Proserpina, to netherworlds. Classical scholars generally place the origins of Greek drama in the mysteries of Eleusis, and indeed Aeschylus eluded the death penalty for revealing some of their secrets only by proving that he had never been initiated into them. I believe that piecing together across time and space this now dimly perceived mosaic will not merely strengthen the historical continuity of literature within itself and with sacred thought but will relate both to modes of knowing—preliterate, literate, and . . . postliterate.

For another example, the double, or doppelgänger, is well recognized, at least since the Romantics, as a literary adaptation of an esoteric concept. Poe's "William Wilson," Dostoyevsky's "The Double," and Conrad's "The Secret Sharer" all feature two characters who at some literal or figurative level represent different aspects of one person. But the double is only a fragment of the esoteric cosmology, according to which the successive emanations create a spectrum of realities, all of which are represented within a human individual as "vehicles" or "bodies" of what we might think of today as different frequencies. The *ka* and *ba* and other Egyptian hieroglyphs that Christian scholars try unsuccessfully to translate with words like "spirit," "shadow," and "soul" denote vehicles in this gradient of vehicles bearing names in Western esoteric literature like "etheric," "astral," "mental" and "causal" bodies. Like the Christian Trinity itself, St. Paul's distinction between the "natural body" and the "spiritual body" represents a truncated exoteric simplification of this spectrum.

The double is the etheric body, just a shade off the regular physical body and therefore perceptible, it is said, to clairvoyant vision, as Carlos Castaneda's shamanic teachers Don Juan and Don Gennaro demonstrated to him on several occasions. The relationships among these vehicles, and the circumstance in which they may split off from each other, as in sleep or trance or trauma, make up a considerable part of esoteric lore. In Karl Miller's *Doubles* (1985), an exhaustive and otherwise valuable treatment of doubles in modern literature, you will find no discussion of esoteric origins beyond the notion in the word doppelgänger itself of a sort of ghost. For a modern description of some of what is typically missing in doubles criticism see A. E. Powell's *The Etheric Body* (1969) or Annie Besant's *Man and His Bodies* (1896, 1960).

The literature of doubles begins with myths of twins like that of Castor and Pollux, one of whom typically is immortal, perhaps the guardian angel to the other, as in "William Wilson," or otherwise depicted as inhabiting a higher plane than the other (the etheric or astral plane). Literary critics tend to regard the use of twins in *The Comedy of Errors* or in its main source, Plautus's *The Menaechmi,* as a plot device to exploit mistaken identity for comic effects, sometimes dark, but the potential seriousness extends beyond the realistic dangers of misunderstanding, and even beyond the psychological symbolism of multiple personalities inhabiting the same body. During the revelations near the end of *Errors,* when the twins come together, Adrian says, "I see two husbands, or mine eyes deceive me." To this the Duke responds: "One of these men is Genius to the other./ And so of these, which is the natural man/ And which the spirit? Who deciphers them?" Here *genius* means *attendant spirit.* Shakespeare knew he was taking over more than just a plot device, and his other plays show understanding of some of the esoteric teaching, most directly dealt with in *The Tempest,* but by his time it was considerably diluted, debased, and fragmented except in certain circles such as the Rosicrucians.

Twins abound in popular fiction and teleplays today, where Jekyll-and-Hyde or multiple-personality symbolism often seems deliberate. But do twins mean still what the zodiacal sign Gemini and the Egyptian *ka* (hieroglyph of double arms) meant to the ancients—the etheric body shadowing the visible body and bespeaking another plane of reality . . . and others beyond that?

Thus esoteric doctrine engenders holy writ like the Hermetica, the Bible, the Vedas, and the first myths, which set in motion forms and processes that evolve and revolve throughout a gradually secularizing literature—themes that are orchestrated and tropes that are encrusted or transformed. The original born-again initiations and the orally transmitted teaching began before writing. The first literature is always poetry because scripture is poetry, and scripture is poetry because only language at once multileveled and incantatory can do justice to the reality it evokes and invokes. For a while it is difficult to tell liturgy from scripture, then canon from apocrypha, or scripture from exegesis. Like Milton's *Paradise Lost* or Shelley's "Endymion," retelling is a form of commentary and reinterpretation. However secular it becomes, literature never severs itself from holy writ, never ceases being apocrypha, because the impact and meaning of any text any time depends on a colossal intertextuality that evolves from one epoch into another and revolves from one culture into another.

More gingerly than I hope will be necessary in the future, two great critics of our day have in some way already taken on this hypothesis—Kenneth Burke in *The Rhetoric of Religion: Studies in Logology* (1961) and Northrop Frye in *The Secular Scripture: A Study of the Structure of Romance* (1976), *Creation and Recreation* (1980), and *The Great Code: The Bible and Literature* (1981). The best way to understand verbalization, Burke says, is to look to theology, the supreme model, because through words referring to the natural world it manages to refer to a supernatural world. From among Frye's complicated analogies between literature and scripture arises also the notion of holy writ as a master code by which to understand language and literature (as Muslims regard the *Koran*). Esoteric doctrine, I believe, is the code to the code, precisely because it is a universal metaphysic underlying the holy writs of various cultures and therefore permeating their gradually secularizing literatures.

Research as Recollection

There is another reason for cultural reexamination and the pursuit of the universalist metaphysic. Except for members of certain organizations like the Association for Moral Education and the Philosophy of Education Society, most educators have avoided issues of moral or spiritual education, though the "laity" often raises them, as in fundamentalist objections to school curriculum and textbooks. Understandably, researchers especially do not want to appear to violate either the separation of church and state or the separation of science from religion. But issues of value underlie research as much as any other activity, as we have seen, and so it would be only honest to include them as part of the subject. The American founding fathers would not have seen the slightest need to separate spirituality from science, since the essence of both is the holistic connectedness of the universe. A main tenet of the esoteric doctrine in which they believed, as Freemasons, is that all things are in correspondence with one another, expressed in "As above, so below" and "I am That." Such expansive identification must surely be a large part of the English teachers' claim that literature educates the moral sensibility.

Researching the hypothesis that literature is a secularization of sacred acts and words—and especially of a universal metaphysic—could clarify and substantiate this claim and could open the way for schools to deal with scripture as scripture, not just as literature, without "teaching religion." By framing literature cosmologically, metaphysically, school can deal with spiritual and religious dimensions while improving the professional offering of literature, which badly needs this dimension. (This of course contrasts with a merely moralistic application of literature to life.) Literature is a cornucopia of diverse riches, but this very profusion affects us more when read against its ultimate ground, which the total intertextuality of scripture and literature itself provides.

What is today called literary criticism has in fact turned sharply in the direction of philosophy and metaphysics and has done so by using cross-disciplinary, cross-cultural knowledge to conduct political, personal, and cultural self-examination. Jacques Derrida has recently focused on Spinoza's theology in relation to the contention that literacy destroys the sacred aspect of language (an issue, incidentally, for Navajos today). A book that caps such trends in typifying fashion is Mark C. Taylor's *Erring: a Postmodern a\Theology* (1984), the title itself expressing how the far-reaching explorations of contemporary literary criticism have brought it back, with perhaps exactly the physicist's ironic ambiguity, to those cosmological considerations that literature secularizes. At any rate, the hypothesis I'm proposing for literature would automatically generate the metaphysical framework within which, it seems to me, researchers should situate themselves anyway for investigating the whole universe of discourse—and other fields of knowing as well.

The American Transcendentalist and innovative educator Bronson Alcott set up a very interesting experiment at his Temple School in Boston. A man who took seriously his cultural inheritance, he taught his pupils by a kind of Socratic dialogue, and the experiment was to test a belief dear to Plato and the whole esoteric transmission—that knowledge is recollection, available from looking within because "I am That." This is one of those "great Western ideas" that advocates of cultural literacy are not apt to list as such, perhaps because they don't believe it squares with science. It accords perfectly, however, with a metaphysic that includes a master force field or cosmic mind having a cosmic memory—like the "reverberating circuits" some neurophysiologists have posited for personal memory—which individuals may access by attunement. In one of the classics of English literature, "Ode: Intimations of Immortality from Recollections of Early Childhood," Wordsworth characterizes the newborn child as "trailing clouds of glory" from the spirit state and "haunted forever by the Eternal Mind."

Alcott asked his students to explain passages from the Gospels on the grounds that, for the very reasons Wordsworth alludes to, they are best qualified to do Biblical exegesis. In 1837 he published his transcriptions as *Conversations with Children on the Gospels.* Even allowing for how his own beliefs about the Gospels must have polluted his research, the children's commentary is remarkable. Community disapproval of the book and of his teaching methods forced Alcott to close the Temple School. But the tradition of knowing as recollecting is a part of cultural heritage that some researchers today are again taking seriously, as Thomas Armstrong makes clear in *The Radiant Child* (1985). Ideas worth transmitting should be worth investigating! Perhaps a child prodigy and an adult genius are just people who have ready access to at least some knowledge that they did not have to learn because their minds attune to what esotericists call the Akashic (Etheric) Record. If we do already know most of what we establish through research, as I speculated at the start, then maybe we are recollecting our knowledge more than we care to admit. Maybe we do research not just to increase what we know but to discover *that* we know.

Part 3

Arranging to Know

The thoughts that follow in this final section of the book represent the very tentative efforts of one person in one field to suggest directions for trying to conceive a sort of unified field theory of learning. Surely everyone wants a *coherent* curriculum. Exactly what sort of *integration* that requires is what has to be determined. And where will this integration take place—in schedules and courses, in learning activities and materials, or in teachers' and students' minds? Indeed, we have to think through the relations among subjects before we can begin to understand, on which plane of action integration should take place.

Educational reform of the 1980s and early 1990s featured institutional restructuring and virtually ignored curriculum itself. Administrative change without curricular change is worse than meaningless—it can lock public education even more tightly into failed ways of organizing learning. The reform agenda of the federal and state governments simply assumed a curriculum comprised of traditional and discrete subjects. The Bush administration's effort to establish a national core curriculum through national assessment, Project 2000, included only math, science, English, geography, and history—not even arts or foreign languages or other social studies. Such an initiative prolongs both the biases and the incoherence of the schooling that is to be reformed.

Subject fields, furthermore, are not of themselves learning fields. They are expedient and logical classifications of content that do not take into account how individuals learn, as is shown in one way by the very fact of their being conceived and purveyed essentially in isolation from each other. For educational purposes, subject fields have to cohere psychologically into a unified learning field structured around how people make or come by knowledge. Such a field would indicate how to restructure administration. And it would extend across the cultural and cosmic fields contemplated so far in this book.

Getting the Subjects Together

Working for the most part independently of each other, the various national school subject organizations began publishing during the late 1980s some books or pamphlets to promulgate as frameworks, guidelines, or standards the latest thinking about how the teaching in their respectives fields should be improved. (See the brief curricular bibliography on page 119.) In 1990 representatives of these subject organizations met to consider the relationships among their new curricular declarations, which were produced without collaboration except between science and math. Having read one another's documents as homework, members formulated at the meeting a joint statement about the commonalities they perceived across subjects and about what was missing. The commonalities amounted to a call for more:

- challenging content and standards for *all* students
- *heterogeneous* grouping of students
- responsiveness to the *diversity* of today's students
- *active* knowledge-making by students
- *collaborative* learning in small groups of students
- assessment of actual *performance,* less multiple choice
- *problem solving* and critical and creative thinking
- learning for *understanding,* less for grades or scores
- selection of *essentials,* less mere coverage
- *student-centered* organization of school time
- *teacher development* and teacher designing of curriculum.

Members considered this amount of convergence remarkable and heartening.

> On the subject of the national education goals put forward by the President and the governors, however, there was no consensus. Some participants felt it would be unwise to identify closely with a highly politicized initiative that might be short-lived. Many were concerned that such identification might suggest an endorsement of a national curriculum. Others felt that the national goals desperately needed professional input that could give them lasting substance. (From page 4 of "The First Curriculum Congress,"an unpublished summary of the first meeting, distributed to members during the fall of 1990.)

The documents did not add up to a complete curricular vision because organizations committed to a particular subject have rarely considered the part that each's subject would play in a total learning experience. This omission of the viewpoint of the learner—for whom all this exists, after all—was a grave deficiency in the documents, as most members realized, and remains a major problem in curriculum reform. The tell-tale fact is that these subject organizations had never met together before to consider the whole curriculum. In 1991 they climaxed a year of periodic meetings by officially organizing the Alliance for Curriculum Reform, whose mission is to play a major role in curriculum reform, reconceptualize the curriculum as a whole, sponsor joint projects, and disseminate effective programs.

It is a measure of the concern for curricular integration that, before the Alliance for Curriculum Reform had finished officially organizing itself, some school districts and state departments of education were already taking steps to replicate it locally by convoking their subject-area representatives to consider the long-range interrelations among their specialities. If such organizations sustain their forums long enough, they will force themselves to take more the learner's viewpoint, to envision a coherent learning environment, and to situate schooling within the broader learning fields of society and nature.

I was a member until members were defined, quite properly, as national organizations only. To witness the wary, ginger way in which these organizations first tried to talk across boundaries and to commit themselves to joint action illuminated for me a good part of the predicament of the curriculum to be reformed. Understandably, the representatives feared subscribing to statements or programs that their constituencies might not agree on enough to ratify. And of course the notion of coalescing subjects in some degree was bound to threaten organizations whose very existence was posited on relatively discrete subject disciplines, as I discovered when I callously introduced the word "fusion" into considerations of integrating the curriculum. For the arts organizations, "integrating the curriculum" has mostly meant absorption into other subjects and loss of integrity, not to mention jobs. But despite this inherent inner conflict, the group took a historic step that may give educators themselves more control over the determination of curriculum in the face of governmental aggression.

The fact that the subject organizations had not been thinking *together* is most disturbing. It means that little work has been done to conceive curriculum as a whole. This is not to discount, however, many fine interdisciplinary projects and relationships that educators have worked on or worked out for many years. English and social studies teachers have jointly taught certain literary works, for example, and of course math is a necessary tool in understanding science. Two organizations represented in the Alliance, in fact, are spearheading the increasing integration of the latter. Project 2061, run by the American Association for the Advancement of Science, is not only integrating math, science, and technology, but working on ties with other subjects as well. And the Mathematical Science Educational Board exists principally to foster this sort of curricular coordination. Though for high school only, Ted Sizer's Coalition of Essential Schools features inquiry across subjects. The Collaborative for Humanities and Arts Teaching (CHART) is a consortium of various interdisciplinary projects funded by the Rockefeller Foundation. As a member during the 1970s of the so-called Faculty of the National Endowment for the Humanities, I had a chance to consult on many interesting school projects that NEH ran to promote some integration across those subjects in their bailiwick.

The very names of most of the above organizations or projects suggest, however, their limitations, though they sometimes test their boundaries. Such agencies and their mandates don't yet extend to *all subjects* for *all times* in *all ways.* Piecemeal efforts need to coalesce into a total learning environment ultimately conceived as such. Educators need to bring the arts and humanities together with the social and natural sciences and these in turn with languages and mathematics and the crafts and vocations.

Within the overriding purpose of providing learners a coherent education, several practical reasons impel us to reconceive the total curriculum with all subjects in mind at once. First of all, there would never be world enough and time to make room in one curriculum for all the subject matter proposed in the separate wish lists of the subject organizations—so many required courses or hours per week in this subject or that, coverage of so many topics in this grade or that. To some extent, such promulgations are just fantasy. Even proliferating electives can't solve this problem, because to offer many of these topics as optional courses would overload the schedule and overtax faculty and resources. Besides, subject specialists want most of their proposed courses or topics to be required, which leads to disputes about priorities among the subjects.

So, second, if some integration of the subjects does not occur, the sciences, math and languages, humanities and arts, vocations and physical education will all fight among themselves for space. America suffers badly from a dearth of knowledge of foreign languages. Business presses hard for math and science. Concern about getting a job warrants vocational courses. A knowledge of history is supposed to prepare the student for participation in a democracy and to further understanding of other peoples. As the hardest to justify in such conventional practical terms, the arts are curtailed first when the budget is cut. The allotment among subjects is endlessly debatable according to equally worthy but competing values. If all are tooting their horns at once without regard for the interrelations among themselves and for the total impact on the learner, some will simply be omitted or mutilated, and the curriculum will continue to be decided by merely invoking some tradition or other, by compromising among special-interest advocacies, and by letting the rest fall out according to the motley contingencies impinging on schools.

Third, the goals of the different subjects overlap considerably, especially in such areas as thinking processes, investigative techniques, and means of proof and evidence. It is not as if only math or only science or only history will teach these; all will. But it's true too that investigation or evidence varies across disciplines according to unique aspects of each discipline. And it might be wise to build some redundance into the learning of such important abilities. But the present unpondered, uncoordinated curriculum does not distinguish happenstance overlap from meaningful redundance. Overall learning is bound to be inefficient so long as it can't benefit from perception about the connections among subjects.

Fourth, the aims and the means proposed in the subject organizations' documents to improve their separate curricula will require more integration with other subjects than the organizations seem prepared for. New math and science guidelines, for example, advocate more realistic problem solving that draws on circumstances and subject matter familiar or important to students. At the same time, the new classroom scenarios play down the preplanned feeding of information according to some internal logic of the subject in favor of more leeway for student timing and discovery. To these emphases add another on student collaboration through small-group processes. If realized, these proposals will tend to replace traditional self-contained courses in math and science with interdisciplinary projects in which math and science are not only coordinated with each other but both in turn melded with humanities, social studies, and arts, since the difficulties of school math and science have concerned, precisely, their remoteness from human feelings and intentions. A group architectural project, for example, could bring all these together so that each could be better learned by allowing their natural interdependencies to become apparent.

In other words, part of what's needed for curriculum reform is an admission that school subjects positively *need* each other, not merely that they have interesting points of contact. The International Reading Association has set an example by publically stating that students can better learn reading comprehension through other subjects than through separate practice reading for its own sake, in which content is indifferent. Similarly, language arts teachers promote "writing across the curriculum," because they know that writing needs the realistic circumstances and authentic subjects and audiences that other subjects can supply. Just as you read and write for reasons that may involve any content whatsoever, you calculate and reason mathematically for purposes that inevitably go outside math itself as a subject. We will consider below this interdependence between languages and the experiential subject matter that languages symbolize.

The organizations representing reading and the other language arts as school subjects welcome curricular integration more than representatives of other subjects do. In fact, they constitute one end of a spectrum ranging from subject organizations least theatened by it to those most threatened by it. The more secure the position of a subject in the curriculum the less worried are its representatives about the possible effects of integration. As a prerequisite for the other "major" subjects, literacy enjoys the highest priority.

Math and science are the next most assured, because they undergird technology and hence the economy, which enlists great political support for them. But note also that math, science, and technology depend too obviously on each other and on literacy for their advocates to contest integration, at least among themselves. History, on the other hand, is a less secure subject, like social studies in general, and its representatives usually resist strenuously any move that would seem to reduce its sovereignty. History remains a required subject only to the extent that it can claim to teach for democracy and world understanding by transmitting American and Western heritages and by acquainting students with other cultures. But this sort of claim can't compete strongly with those of the preceding subjects. As basic practical knowledge, geography fares well only for a while in elementary school, like the other social sciences, which inherently interest young people but which barely exist in the curriculum beyond childish stereotyping. Foreign languages are rarely required in school, and most schools can't find or afford enough foreign language teachers to staff either a required or an elective program. The fact is that America is a big island where little need is felt for foreign languages, and, abroad, English has practically become the lingua franca. Accustomed to not commanding much urgency except for college admission, foreign language educators are not so much threatened by integration as resigned to a low priority.

Most threatened are arts educators, who are traumatized by decades of seeing their subjects slighted, deleted, incorporated, or made adjunct to subjects enjoying secure dominion in the curriculum. The arts are at the losing end of the subject spectrum because personal development ranks low among the various goals invoked to justify subjects. Clearly, the degree of threat that curricular integration poses to educators is directly proportional to the strength of their subject's place in the curriculum—how much of it is required or offered according to the mostly utilitarian standards preferred by government and business.

This spectrum is a value scale. In the squabbling for curricular space that constitutes a major theme in the history of modern common schooling, educators have kept trying to argue that their subject fulfills one or more of the handful of justifications that this society warrants for school inclusion. Thus when Latin could no longer be justified on the old grounds, it was then alleged to teach thinking, always a good rationale. Likewise, history teaches logical inference, we're told (and I accept), through the rules of evidence and proof (whereas a better justification in kids' minds would be that it's full of appalling and appealing stories). Literature is supposed to refine the moral sensibility. This strikes close to that old goal of making good citizens, which learning about "our" heritage of freedom will also further. Math and science will, nationally, increase the industrial and economic productivity and, personally, get you a good job. These utilitarian justifications, which make up most school goals, barely rise above political sloganeering. Personal development or fulfillment figures among these justifications but usually near the end of the list and clearly, as the spectrum above shows, at the bottom of school priorities.

Part of why we need to rethink the total curriculum is to reconsider these justifications and their underriding values. If, for example, math and science were construed more humanistically and taught in closer relationship to other subjects, they might further personal growth as much as they might the gross national product. Most often, one chooses to study a foreign language for personal reasons. And recognized as modes of cognition, the arts may teach thinking as much as the other subjects. The question, in other words, of how much a subject is worth depends not only on the society's professed values but also on how the subject is ultimately understood, in depth, in consideration with other subjects. Educators have to take a big step back and ask, "What part does my subject, or might my subject, play in personal development and social evolution—in consciousness and culture?" But each educator is not going to be able to answer this without pondering it with colleagues in other subjects. As it is, schooling is running on a lot of dead assumptions about the subjects based on historical fallout, governmental pressure, bureaucratic distortion, and . . . the absence of a *learner* advocacy to put the subject advocacies in their places within a total learning enterprise.

The professional subject organizations are in a position similar to that of modern nations fearing to yield some sovereignty and identity to an international governance but participating in global economic or ecological activities that any one of them cannot deal with adequately within its own jurisdiction. Trying to maintain the old boundaries contradicts somewhat the higher aims and the more realistic methods that the recent curricular documents rightly advocate. A continuous forum about the total curriculum carried on among educators in all subjects, such as the one instigated by the Alliance for Curriculum Reform, will gradually bring out many unexploited and even unsuspected ways in which traditional subjects can help each other realize their goals. In fact, it is in the nature of the best education that it can't happen without some greater integration than institutions of learning now permit of the arts, sciences, languages, humanities, crafts, and vocations. However expedient it may be for institutional and professional purposes to apportion knowledge and knowledge making into departments, no school reform effort will succeed if it doesn't acknowledge how these artifactual subject divisions thwart the naturally integrative functioning of individual thought.

Finally, the master argument for curricular integration is simply that life is not divided into subjects. This argument may be grounded in either personal or social reality. That is, academic departments fit neither the way individuals build their personal knowledge structures nor the way societal problems arise to which knowledge may be applied. Learning and doing cut across at myriad angles the subject areas established by universities for purposes of scholarship, research, and accreditation—divisions that no longer accommodate well even those ends. For precisely these realistic reasons, that both inner and outer life intermix subjects, language educators now believe it's better to integrate listening, speaking, reading, and writing; science educators, biology, chemistry, physics, and earth sciences; arts educators, drama, music, dance, and art; math educators, arithmetic, algebra, geometry, and calculus. Perhaps it's time to intermix these major subjects themselves.

The threat that merging poses can be justly offset by not only looking for commonalities and overlap and significant "fits" among the subjects but also by insisting on searching for the uniqueness of each, for what it does or offers that makes it complement other subjects and fulfill an individual's education as nothing else can. Uniquenesses will help us consider what we mean by "integrate." We can imagine a spectrum of kinds of integration going from subjects being barely tangent to their being virtually congruent. It may be that for some learning purposes integration will mean merely *interrelating distinct subjects* so as to make them reveal each other better. Or it may mean *softening some boundaries between them* for a time in order to accommodate the personal and social nature of learning, which is not necessarily subject-oriented. Or it may mean *smelting all subjects down together and recasting them as a single curriculum.*

Which form of integration is appropriate no doubt depends partly on child development and on personal maturation. Schools are forced to be child-centered in primary school and to center on discrete subjects only gradually. Interestingly, the learning slump referred to earlier occurs about the same time that schools start to break learning into math, science, social studies, language arts, and other arts. When, in middle school, subjects are allocated to separate classrooms and separate teachers, student centering yields so thoroughly to institutional anonymity that many students never recover and nearly all shrink their minds to the constraints of the situation.

Howard Gardner (1985) has suggested that child development may alternate between specialized and generalized knowledge according to five periods of the first half of life. Like other concepts of child development, this would most likely be translated into curriculum in group terms, that is, as all children alternating at the same time. Gardner himself seems to imply a rough synchronization of children of the same age, but it is the failure to individualize child development that has caused schools to misuse such research. Not only may children arrive at the same stages at different ages but their personal histories and individual penchants may count for more in their educational needs than a generic pattern of "child development," which in any case these personal factors may modify considerably.

So the quest for the appropriate degree of integration—from casual cross-reference to fusing crucible—must consider not only a developmental dimension along time but the accommodation of individualized learning. Those experimental private schools or alternative public schools that best serve as some sort of beacons for school reform have found ways to pluralize curriculum—to think of *the* curriculum as a learning field in which to work out individualized *curricula* that differ from student to student. In other words, the matter of how to integrate the subjects is partly a factor of how to make up personal programs according to particular knowledge structures each individual is building and according to the modes of knowing each tends toward. Understanding the nature of the subjects and of their interrelationships cannot be separated from understanding the nature of learners as individuals.

Individualized learning and an integrated curriculum are inherently related, because the perspective of the overall learning field correponds to the viewpoint of the learner, whose growth moves forward on all fronts and all planes simultaneously all the time. The chief issue concerns assimilation—how kinds of new knowledge become structured into the old and into each other, given that this must occur in unpredictable individual ways. How do you do this so as to preserve the integrity of both the subject and of the individual? Traditional schooling has far overfavored the integrity of the subject, as with full-year courses in algebra or biology or American history that present the subject self-contained according to its internal logic but that are difficult to assimilate. These can be admirably cogent and elegant but equally indigestable and forgettable. The real test here is how many students have got good grades in such courses but remembered or applied little of the material later.

All we alumni and alumnae take this loss for granted and even joke about it the way we do other commonalities of schooling or growing up, but this chronic bad timing or unassimilability explains the inefficiency of schooling as much perhaps as any single factor. Presenting subject matter self-consistently, to a generic student body, in large prescheduled blocks, bores and boggles students, to whom this all appears arbitrary. In other words, to sacrifice the psychology of the learner to the logic of the subject is to jeopardize not only the meaning the subject may have for the student but the meaning the subject may have for the specialist as well. The subject may be public knowledge, but for better or worse, the learner digests it personally.

So if only to make individualization possible, or if only to take the learner's point of view, or if only to think coherently about total education reform, we must at least *consider* smelting down conventional subjects and methods and, without losing anything of value unique to any of them, recasting the whole learning process as fundamentally and universally as possible. Again, the place and form of this recasting remain to be determined by much deliberation. Somewhere in this exploration we can perhaps discover how to do justice to the integrity of both the student and the subject. Maybe they will never be other than factors of each other. Maybe those students most honor the integrity of the subject who learn it most personally. At any rate, suppose we approach the known and the knower as inseparable, as in Yeats's question, "How can we tell the dancer from the dance?"

Verbal and Nonverbal Learning

The curriculum should integrate such wordless learning as arts and crafts, and physical and practical activities, with discursive or academic learning, which needs to be both counterbalanced and nourished by nonverbal learning, for the sake of the total development of the individual. Besides, intelligence operates through many modalities—sensory, kinesthetic, spatial, and emotional—that feed in and out of each other and the verbal mode. Finally, academic subjects have practical applications to various vocations that, in return, supply the realistic problems and circumstances that educators now say best help students understand the subjects.

How do verbal and nonverbal learning interplay? This question should hang before us constantly as we go about integrating the curriculum. Except for sports, shop, and home economics, which are so sharply separated from academic subjects as to form almost a separate curriculum, schools have seldom bothered much about learning divorced from language. Most traditional subjects are cast into language and cannot be learned without words. Literature, history, and most math and science are taught mainly through texts and talk.

By contrast, playing a piano or making a puppet requires sensory and kinesthetic skills. But virtually no sort of learning is purely verbal or nonverbal if you consider it fully; some aspects of math are visual—like graphs and geometric shapes—and the information of the natural and social sciences builds on observation of wordless phenomena. On the other side, verbal coaching is a part of most sports and crafts, and learning to read music is usually, at some stage, part of learning to play a piano or trumpet.

Schools have made some subjects more verbal than they should be in order to format them into standard courses with books and lectures and have made students such passive information receivers that "book l'arnin' " seems to be about all that's required. Viewed only as content, as amassed bodies of information, science and social studies appear almost entirely bookish. To the extent they are construed, however, as the investigative processes by which knowledge in these fields is *made,* then sensory, kinesthetic, and intuitive learning are definitely also in order, though not favored by public education because student investigation seems hard to organize and control within the conventional school framework.

According to a bias of our culture and therefore of our schools, thinking is mostly or entirely verbal, that is, it depends on words. Or if nonverbal thinking exists, it's concrete and hence not very important. One could make a very good case that the really important thinking is nonverbal, because the most original ideas come from intuition and are cast first in a form of feeling or imagery that only later takes on the labels and structure of language (which tends to standardize thought). We usually assume that if a lot of language is being used, a lot of thinking must be going on. But it's clear that words can be used to avoid thinking or to control the thought of others—both serious problems in mass institutions. Students should read and write vastly more than they do, but making literacy second nature should not be confused with reducing education to book learning.

Students need to interact directly with the things of the world that prompt thoughts, the social and natural environments, from which public education actually insulates youngsters by segregating and immobilizing them off in special buildings. The minds even of lower animals atrophy without plentiful stimulation. No matter how provocative a teacher or textbooks might conceivably become, they could never provide the thinking fields that real environments can. Learners need to exchange with nature and society, and public education has to arrange for them to do this.

At the same time that students are learning to cast this experience into ordinary and mathematical language, they should be practicing the nondiscursive arts such as film, painting, music, and dance. To think is to perceive relations. This may be done with and without words, in various media, sometimes rationally, sometimes intuitively. Surely education must include alternative ways to have thoughts and to cast thoughts. The best curriculum would enable learners to interconnect things as much as possible by keeping all subjects, media, and modes of knowing in play all the time. But it shouldn't make the connections itself. The one who does *that* is the one who's thinking.

Languages and Subjects

To integrate the curriculum, we have to understand the differences across which we are connecting. Some school "subjects" are not really subjects at all but *languages,* by means of which we can discourse about *any* subject. So let's make a major distinction between content subjects and languages, but only in order to relate them anew. As languages, Spanish and English and mathematics differ entirely from subjects based on material content like government, economics, history, chemistry, and psychology, which are both bodies of accumulated information and disciplines of ongoing investigation. (It's in a different sense—metacognitive—that English or math can also be said to have bodies of content and disciplines of investigation.) By treating languages and subjects alike—formatting and teaching them in similar "courses"—schools have made all "subjects" harder to learn in themselves and to relate to each other.

The difference between languages and subjects is precisely what relates them. Languages symbolize subjects. This relation of symbolizer to symbolized should inform the whole curriculum. To the extent subjects are cast into language, students have to learn the language and the subjects together. Languages, for their part, can't in fact be learned without some subject matter as wherewithal to symbolize. Sensing this but hell-bent nevertheless to teach English and math as separate "subjects" like the others, schools have trumped up arbitrary material to exercise with, "topics" for composition and "story problems" for calculation.

English courses have made a monster out of grammar and spoiled literature by commandeering these in the misguided search for a specialized content when any subject matter whatsoever will serve as something to talk, read, and write about. The main thing is that the material should involve the hearts and minds of the learners sufficently for them to practice these language arts realistically. In drawing their subject matter from experience, students are in fact dealing with people and nature anyway and therefore working with traditional curricular topics now allotted to courses in social studies and the sciences.

Math courses have suffered from a virtual absence of any subject matter except math's own rules of operation. It is mainly this disconnection from nature and people that maintains the famous mental block on math shared by most Americans, because the main school problem with math is its abstractness. By its nature, abstraction disembeds objects from their familiar context in order to consider only one aspect or quality of them. By abstracting only the quantitative aspect of things, math operates so high up in the realm of pure logic that most people can't relate to it except through the medium of some familiar content.

Without a subject matter other than itself to operate on, furthermore, math does not come across as a language or symbol system, certainly not one to use in everyday life. Good texts and teachers have of course always tried to show something of how math can be applied, but this is too time-consuming to do much of within the framework of a course obligated to cover certain math "content" like algebra and geometry, and these sample applications just reinforce the arbitrariness of the rest of the canned curriculum. Like English, math needs to be practiced constantly in direct relationship to the familiar phenomena of life. The curricular movement called "reading and writing across the curriculum" tries to wed languages and subjects in just this way but cannot surmount the doggedly held school practice of segregating all of the languages and subjects into separate courses.

What Languages Share

Mathematical symbols and expressions can be spoken, read, and written. These symbols are variously combined to "spell" the equivalent of words, which are in turn variously combined into the expressions that compare to phrases, which are in turn predicated into formulas and equations that make statements like sentences. Math and English can be translated into each other—at least up to the point where ordinary language can no longer keep up with the greater abstraction and finer logical precision of mathematics, which are of course what require the different symbols and syntax. Perhaps we should think of math as a special sort of second language but one learned very early.

What ordinary and mathematical languages basically share is logic embodied in vocal and written symbols. Math is a purer form of logic that extends ordinary language into a higher range of abstraction. Whereas English, say, starts by *naming* physical objects and concrete experiences, math starts by *numbering* them. Both refer at first to the familiar world, but referring to the qualities of things keeps ordinary language much closer to this world than referring only to the quantities of things, as math does. Continuous on an abstractive spectrum, the qualitative and quantitative languages complement each other beautifully.

This complementarity reflects the human brain's dual approach to codifying reality. By interrelating the qualities and quantities of things, people make knowledge. Nothing could be more important for education than coordinating the development of these two kinds of language. This can be done by applying both, at once and all the time, to the topical subjects.

Seriation

Consider also that writing began with recording, which consisted of *1–2-3*'s, as well as *a-b-c*'s. In antiquity the letters of alphabets long served for numbers, as early writers registered both counts and acts. The first writing seems to have been a form of book*keeping,* so that earlier people identified storytelling with counting.

The word *bookkeeping* itself refers to a book in the sense of a ledger. The double meaning of *book* exactly matches the double meaning of *account.* In a story book we give an account of some events, and in a ledgerbook we keep accounts of numerical transactions. Vestiges of this identification between tales and tallies are fixed in the language. In Keats's "Eve of St. Agnes" the fingers of the holy man "told his rosary," that is, counted the beads to tally his prayer repetitions. In other languages than just English, telling is recounting, as in the French *raconter* or German *erzahlen.* Why did our forebears treat these as intrinsically connected?

Today we may be used to thinking of numbers as very different from words—figures from figures of speech. But narrating and numbering have in common something terribly fundamental—serial order.

Chronology is the order in which events happen, the very definition of time. The fact that *this* act happened before *that* one is not to be tampered with. Start in the middle of the story, if you like, as Homer did, and flash back to earlier events, but do that only to make more, not less, out of what came first, next, and last. Without their serial order numbers too lose meaning. What "prior" and "later" are to narrating, "more than" and "less than" are to numbering. In any sense of "tell" it's essential to get the sequence right.

Without seriation, a number is just one primitive way of clustering things that seem alike—five nuts, five fingers, or the number of sheep matched off with pebbles dropped in a bowl as they pass into the pen. By itself a number is just a class of things, threeness or twelveness. Without seriation you can't say or learn anything more about this class because it is not in relationship. A number not ordered can't even be added, subtracted, multiplied, or divided. Where does it stand? It's a noun that can't be put into a sentence. A number *series,* on the other hand, starts to supply predicates in the very idea of "before" and "after."

Even the notion of causation seems built on sequence, as we can see in the double meaning of "since" as either "after" or "because," of "while" as "during" or "whereas." Our language and our thinking chronically blur temporal and logical sequence, as in our notion of "what follows." A "conclusion" may come after the climax of either a sequence of events or a chain of logic. What goes before seems to determine what comes after, as we can see somewhat comically in even the technical term "entailment" from symbolic logic.

The what-happened-next of "then . . . then" leads quite comfortably to the "if . . . then" of reasoning. The stages are marked by sentences like "If you allow water in the gasoline, the engine sputters" (cause-and-effect time sequence) and "If the other two angles in a right triangle are equal, they are 45 degrees each" (a relating of measurements). Here "if" is almost interchangeable with time-space words like "whenever" or "wherever."

It's easy to understand how sequences of events could become synonymous with causes and effects, but a number series seems too mechanical to be parallel to causation. But actually, each number is not merely like the one before it except larger. Across the steady beat of one more being added to the previous number there fall various counterbeats that create different rhythms.

To begin with, every other number in the whole number series is odd and alternates with even numbers, which can be divided in half. Three is not merely one more than two but a prime, or indivisible, number in the subseries 3, 5, 7, 11, 13, 17, etc. Four is not merely one more than three but a square number in the subseries 9, 16, 25, 36, etc. Six is not merely one more than five but the first in the subseries of "perfect" numbers, each of which is the sum of its factors ($1 \times 2 \times 3 = 1 + 2 + 3$). The famous Fibonacci series (1, 2, 3, 5, 8, 13, etc.), formed by adding two adjacent numbers, beginning with 1 and 1, to obtain the next number ($1 + 1 = 2$, $1 + 2 = 3$, $2 + 3 = 5$, $3 + 5 = 8$, $5 + 8 = 13$), corresponds to certain ratios in geometry and biology. What is the frequency or pattern by which prime or square or perfect or Fibonacci numbers crop up within the whole numbers series? (With some exceptions the prime numbers fit between the square numbers.) These subseries ripple across each other in fascinating relationships and sometimes also express phenomena in the material world.

Since position in the number series determines the quantity and hence the traits of a given number and how it may relate to others, this determination might be compared to some sorts of causation in stories by which earlier events are held to "entail" or "lead to" later ones. Like the chronological order of before and after, the numerical order of more than and less than generates out of its simplicity a more complicated conceptual overlay. This occurs because both chronology and number contain a secreted logic that manifests only across some extended segment of their respective seriations. In math it generates periodicities, intervals, and progressions that have intrigued mathematicians since antiquity, as they can students, who also enjoy puzzles and surprising revelations.

Limitations of Language

Seriation is of course only one aspect of the linearity of language that math and English share. The sequence in which words or mathematical expressions are placed generally makes a difference, though both systems allow some leeway or options in order. More important, the statements made in both sorts of language proceed step by step, from sentence to sentence or equation to equation. They feed ideas to us cumulatively, so that each adds something to its predecessors. Consecutive processing has its limits, however, which is why one hemisphere of the brain specializes in handling material simultaneously.

One reason why education must honor nonverbal learning is to offset the limitations of languages, of which linearity is one. A tune spins out one after another the same notes that its chord sounds simultaneously. The tune is a plural version of the unity of the chord. You do not fully know the notes until you hear them sounded together as well as separately. Full knowledge combines both melody and harmony, succession and simultaneity, plurality and unity, both hemispheres of the brain.

But tunes and chords don't merely balance each other. A chord is a matrix from which many tunes may be generated by permuting the notes in various orders. All melodies so derived share the tonal qualities of the chord—its particular set of intervals—and yet differ from one another by virtue of stringing differently the same notes.

These melodies amount to different statements, even different interpretations, of the same matrix or matter. They are like sentences about a subject.

Statements in language, like melodies, can only partially render the matter, because if more than one sequence is possible, then any sequence represents a preference, a value judgment. One might try to do justice to the potentialities of the chord or other matter by deriving multiple melodies or statements from it, but if presented simultaneously these would create cacophany. Besides, in some cases the number of melodies or statements might be virtually infinite.

But we are not dealing here merely with sequence alone, which is meaningless without considering the individual values of the notes or words being sequenced. Just as each note has a certain frequency and duration that interplays with neighboring notes, words have certain meanings that combine syntactically to produce cumulative effects. Short sequences like phrases are sequenced into longer units or statements that are in turn sequenced into complete musical or written compositions. But all this organization of successions succeeds only because the basic units—notes and words—have individual value and meaning that collectively express the plurality of the world. Sequencing, in other words, requires some particles to be sequenced and hence presupposes some breakdown of whole into parts. A melody analyzes a chord into its constituent notes. Language distorts life not only by processing it sequentially but by fragmenting it into artificial particles in order to do so.

Moreover, the concepts embodied in words are human-made and cut up life into "things" or "actions" that falsify its parts and obscure its unity. The world itself is wordless, unconceptual, nonverbal. In talking about the world we strip out only some aspects from its infinite possibilities, some that interest us. To perceive is to select, and to verbalize perception is to confine it to the finite, ready-made concepts of vocabulary. The number of words, of concepts, nowhere near equals all the possible perceptions of things. Furthermore, not just the concepts are limited. The ways in which we can predicate our little stock of concepts into statements falls dangerously short of rendering the infinite intricacies of the nonverbal world. Syntax suffers from the same crudity and partiality as vocabulary.

For these and other reasons, language cannot match reality. This truth applies no more to the nuances of sensibility than to the subtleties of matter and energy. The more we can acknowledge this truth, the less it is a problem. The problem arises from thinking that everything can be said. But traditional schooling has been far too unsophisticated to acknowledge the limits of discursive knowledge. In fact, it has tended to glorify verbalism and bookishness to the point of actually undermining language, which can't be mastered without understanding its imperfect relationship to the nonverbal reality it's basically about.

What language can and cannot do is best learned, moreover, by practicing it alongside nonverbal media such as film, painting, dance, and music. More even than in the past, schools shunt the arts aside as frills that take time away from "basic skills." This is the kind of ignorance that the curriculum passes down because the fusion of all its subjects has never been sought for and thought out. Of course students should practice all the arts for their own sake, not merely to compare them with language, but in allowing students to connect all things with each other, curricular integration naturally enables them to find out how the various media complement one another. The graphic and lively arts symbolize experience too; they too make and transmit knowledge. Schools have to get over the idea that the arts just entertain and must accept them as *alternative modes of knowing.* Not all knowledge is discursive, and without the context of these alternatives we don't know what to make of discourse itself.

Languages have ways of escaping their own limitations, but to understand these we have to refer the language arts to the other arts. Art connects the verbal with the nonverbal and provides language the means to correct itself in some measure. For this point let's resume the search for what languages share.

Transformations

Both mathematical and ordinary languages feature alternative ways of symbolizing something. They do so not for the sake of mere versatility but because putting the same thing in different ways allows us to think about it differently. This is essential to developing ideas and minds.

Any definition that's of use, for example, tells you what something means by recasting it in other terms you may already understand. Dictionaries define a word by supplying us one or more synonyms for it, by giving us a phrase that's equivalent, or by explaining it in a sentence. All these ways of defining put the same thing in different words, which in logic is called tautology. A great deal of talk and writing consists of defining, which may elaborate an object or idea or bring out its details and implications. Sometimes authors spend whole paragraphs, essays, or books defining something. Much of our discourse puts something another way in order "to go into it."

The equivalent in math of definition is equation. Some expression on the right side of the equal sign recasts what is on the left. The equation $25 = 75/3$ puts 25 in other terms so as to bring out some aspect of it not evident in its initial form, namely, that it's the same as one third of 75. To bring out some other implications, we might write $25 = 4^2 + 3^2$, an equation which reveals that the square of 5 comprises the squares of its two antecedents in the whole-number series, 4 and 3—a very different definition of 25 indeed.

Most mathematical operations occur through series of equations that end in something very different from the beginning. By stating that *this* is really the same as *that,* which in turn is another way of expressing something else, and so on, a series of equations keeps recasting terms until they yield an "answer," that is, some form of the original that is desirable. Besides the solving-for-x type of vertical series of equations that students are familar with, there is the horizontal sort where the right-hand side of an equation simply becomes the left-hand side of another equation in an open-ended continuity that follows out the implications of the first formulation as far as one can or wants.

The second, or open-ended, series of transformations is really a sequence of logical deduction that starts with a kind of premise, the original formulation, and parlays this in stages to some unforeseen conclusion that is a new truth latent in the original expression but not apparent except through the transformations. This is tautology at work, and it is the essence of math, but in less pure form it is central also to ordinary language.

Syllogisms, for example, work much like series of equations. If statement A is true, and if statement B is also true, then what else must "follow," must be true as well? If lowering taxes encourages people to spend, and if spending strengthens the economy, then lowering taxes strengthens the economy. The conclusion restates the first two statements, the "givens," just as the right-hand side of an equation reformulates the original formulation on the left. In both cases these logical chains may continue very far indeed and end in startling discoveries even though no new factual information has been introduced. Such is the power of logic.

Besides definitions and syllogisms, the tautology of ordinary language works in another way, one that can enable it to escape somewhat its own limitations. This is metaphor, which also puts things another way so that we can see them differently. If we refer to a tree as a sentinel, we are setting up an equation that brings out new aspects of the tree. Suddenly we see it as protective and exposed, like a soldier posted alone to stand watch over others. Like equations, metaphors tranform some given thing by selectively cuing off of certain of its qualities. Gerard Manley Hopkins begins a poem, "Glory be to God for dappled things" and then likens a number of speckled and checkered things to one another. He thus creates a new class that cuts across conventional categories and reorders our mind, as creative equations do.

At the same time, metaphor offsets the linearity of language by referring simultaneously to more than one thing, since an equation like tree/sentinel has at least two terms. Figurative works of literature may thus tell a story and make a statement at the same time or, like *Moby Dick,* simultaneously tell several stories and make several statements by building up a rich complex of metaphor. A metaphor like the white whale keeps acquiring referents as its increasingly denser context places it in association with more and more things. Each of Moby Dick's traits—its whiteness, its gargantuan size, its ferocity, its adaptation to the sea—come to stand for associated qualities in humanity and the environment, so that whenever Moby Dick is referred to, these qualities are also referred to and cross-referred among themselves. This multiple reference resembles a musical chord: just as plural notes are sounded together when a chord is struck, plural meanings are indicated at once when the metaphor is mentioned.

Thus tautology can allow a language to undo itself. This possibility is inherent in putting something another way, because once you have equivalence—two or more things assigned equal value—you are only a step away from equivocation—two or more things assigned the same symbol. This simultaneity offsets the linearity of the consecutive words and statements. In linking together disparate things by certain shared aspects, metaphor restores the unity of the nonverbal world that language otherwise fragments.

Nonverbal Aspects

Language has its nonverbal aspects, then, and metaphor is one of them. Creating metaphors partakes of a general mental capacity for seeing likenesses that does not depend on language. I'm sure that before human beings developed speech they likened other objects to each other on the basis of one or another shared trait. And even most animals can recognize a new instance of some creature or object because it looks *like* other instances they have seen previously. This requires some capacity to cognize similitude, which is the basis of metaphor, as indeed it is of all classification.

However much we may associate metaphor with language and literature, this classifying capacity belongs to thinking before it does to speaking. Words stand for classes of things and usually derive—metaphorically—from names for concrete objects. And the use of metaphor makes up a goodly part of the art of literature. Imagery in general plays a major role in writing, but physical vision is not verbal merely because it can be verbalized. Figures of speech are just figures before they are figures of speech.

Language can overcome its verbal limitations to the extent that by its nature it includes nonverbal elements. Both ordinary and mathematical languages refer to physical things, though math does so much more abstractly through its quantification and its idealized geometrical shapes. The nonverbal world necessarily influences languages because the function of languages is to symbolize reality so we can make our way in it. Of course languages are structured to fit the human mind that creates them, but they also have to accommodate what they symbolize. What they fit well about the nonverbal world is its pluralism, the profusion of nature.

Hence ordinary language features the diverse qualities, the many traits by which we cut up the world into classes of things that we name with words and relate into sentence statements. Math does justice to the pluralism by counting and measuring things and then by laying these counts and measures over against each other in various ways such as ratios and equivalences. Though qualifying and quantifying inhere more in the mind than in the objects symbolized, they do reflect with some fidelity this material profusion of the environment with which people have to deal. In fact, it must be the case that human beings are outfitted in the first place with these capacities to qualify and quantify precisely because we need them to map our way amid the prodigality of nature. The ordinary and mathematical languages are capable of such sophisticated operations that they can in some measure correct for their own distortion. In the hands of great logicians and poets these languages seem to render reality justly despite the limitations of discursive media—at least to the satisfaction of the current culture. But truth has a way of evolving with the culture. Logic may be a basic human faculty and math a universal language, but logic can be put into the service of the most parochial or partisan enterprises, and if deduction starts with partial premises it will not arrive at impartial conclusions.

Knowing the world only via symbols is dangerous, because the essential dynamism of nature can't be known that way. Many languages themselves acknowledge this by specifying two different verbs of knowing, such as *connaître* and *savoir* in French and *kennen* and *wissen* in German. The first of each pair means to know directly from experience, as to know a person or a place, to be acquainted with, whereas the second means to know intellectually, as a fact, to know *that* something is so. Language can do nothing for the direct, experiential knowledge and can even get in the way of it, but at least it can talk about it, as I am doing here, and thus bend back upon itself and become a metalanguage to in some way counter itself.

But of course nothing substitutes for nonverbal experience. Language creates verbal circles that seem true because they are self-consistent. And because words refer to things, they delude us into believing that what they say about things is necessarily true. Language refers to itself as much as to things outside itself. To some extent it represents the mind talking to itself. The truths it formulates about reality are always a "manner of speaking," biased by the cerebrality that created discourse. Thoroughly understanding this, as even very few well educated people do, makes the difference between being the master or the dupe of language.

The abstractive process of symbolizing is both valuable and dangerous. Any medium—verbal or nonverbal—will refract reality according to its particular nature. Language is no exception. Nothing could be more important for students to learn than this double-edged potential of symbolization. This is why the entire curriculum must keep the gains and losses of each medium constantly in the learner's consciousness. Truly integrated learning puts all media in play all the time, without prejudice, so that learners find out what each of the alternative symbolizations—language arts, graphic arts, and lively arts—can and cannot do.

But of course this works only if learners can interact at the same time with the material and social worlds that these media symbolize. By insulating young people for twelve or sixteen years or more in a verbal world, schools have not only cut off the academic subjects themselves from the nonverbal material they're founded on but have distorted through the lens of symbolization the nature of reality itself. Professors and school teachers are wordmongers because they make a living essentially through talk and books, which, moreover, accommodate institutional controls very well when directed from the top down, as in schools. This bent may make it especially hard for educators to right the imbalance in schools between the verbal and nonverbal. But we cannot understand language itself without silence, much less the silent world it symbolizes. Learners simply must experience life part of the time unmediated by culture, which, God knows, has its say through not only language but through a society's whole "cake of custom."

Even in the most hard-bitten culture of poverty where few people read and most are forced to confront some realities very directly indeed, people are still imprisoned in the conceptual cage of the local society. In fact cultures of poverty perpetuate, notoriously, a narrow view of the world. Many teachers may say, "Well, my job is to give students language; they get all the nonverbal experience they can deal with out of school." But people who use language less are no less bound by the oral culture they grow up in. Actually, their thought is more limited because they don't develop language to the point where it mitigates its limitations, *nor* do they acquire the broader nonverbal experience that the affluent enjoy. The disadvantaged need more of both, and if this is to be provided during the formative years, public education will have to arrange for it.

The problem for learners of any economic level is how to compare social versions of reality with nonverbal experience of it and thus how to sort out culture from the rest of nature. This is not a neat matter, because people become acculturated so early and so thoroughly that even when experiencing the nonverbal world "directly," they are in fact peering at reality through a cultural filter, which they have internalized along with the language and other social behavior. Traditional schooling sacrifices the truth quest for social knowledge deemed to be more practical. But culture is humanly fallible and without the self-awareness that comes from standing outside itself drifts into the most impractical conditions, including self-destruction. Culture must evolve to save itself. It will only if the young can see through it enough to change it. This means slipping the limits of discourse, which are locked into the limits of culture.

What Subjects Share

Though they differ in what they are *about*—in their information—government, economics, history, chemistry, and psychology share some common processes for making their information, for investigating. These are processes of observing and reasoning that characterize the human mind and determine how we make and store knowledge, although each field has its own concepts and frameworks that influence in turn how its practitioners observe and reason.

Methods of Investigation

All the knowledge studied in schools as social studies and the natural sciences or, say, as nursing or economics was constructed and is still being constructed by common ways of investigating and interpreting that learners should practice themselves. Public education has preferred to emphasize *what* a field has established rather than *how* practitioners in the field come by this knowledge. A bureaucracy can much more easily purvey to students the established content of a field than it can let them experience the investigative process by which that content becomes established. Authentic inquiry doesn't fit the passive stance that schools keep students in for control purposes or the manipulative managerial systems built into the canned commercial curricula prevailing in schools.

But content is only part of the "subject," as professionals in the field would be the first to say. Students should of course learn as much as possible of the information and concepts of biology or anthropology, but they should also do some version of the investigation that the practitioners do. In fact, role-playing professionals is one of the best ways to learn the content, because investigators have to situate their project within what is already known.

To investigate something, you go and look at it, go and ask about it, or go look it up. If what you want to know can't be found out by observing somewhere, asking someone, or consulting some sort of documents like books or films that store information, then you set up an experimemt, that is, some special circumstances, so you can have something to observe not otherwise available. Investigative journalists routinely do all of these except perhaps experiment. They visit, they interview, and they read or view what previous investigators have found out. Like researchers in the social and natural sciences, they may combine all of these or, depending on the project, utilize only one. Folklorists may attend ceremonies or interview oldtimers or look up archives.

These methods are basic because the environment and other people are the main sources of information. What have people found out before you? What do you need to see for yourself? Sometimes living individuals know what you want to know. Sometimes the information is collectively known and has been pooled in repositories. Students should learn these basic firsthand and secondhand methods, including experimentation, and employ them for inquiry into both new and established subjects. Becoming an investigator yourself changes utterly how you may feel about and assimilate the contents of traditional school subjects. In addition, the more students feel that these basic processes of inquiry constitute a common denominator for all subjects, the more they can integrate knowledge themselves.

Chemistry or biology, government or sociology, also share with each other—and with typing, computer programming, and nursing—the possibility of practical application in, say, curing disease or improving the national economy or giving psychotherapeutic counseling. So besides being distillations of acquired knowledge and procedures for increasing that knowledge, the true "subjects" feed their knowledge into the marketplace and world of emerging affairs. Application too is part of what a student learning a subject should find out about that subject.

Whether "academic" or "vocational," any field of knowledge has political and economic implications that young people should become aware of. Consider how rapidly discoveries in genetics become technology, which in turn becomes business, all the while raising legal and moral issues. Or consider how sexism and certification in nursing affect what may be known in the field and indeed how the field is defined. Typically, schools have avoided sensitive issues that might arouse complaints from some interest groups and have pretended to an impossible neutrality.

But schools don't have to take or avoid a stand on controversial matters. All they have to do is teach students to investigate the environment, to think for themselves by visiting the sites, interviewing the practitioners, and reviewing the literature concerned with these fields and issues. As a matter of fact, this is also an excellent way for young people to research career possibilities. Apprenticing of course also permits investigating a subject as it's applied. People and places concretize a subject for learners—impel them to learn both the content of a field and the role it plays in society.

The young need to "enter the world" long before they leave school and seek a job. Keeping students naive and ignorant of what we do with knowledge is one way schools infantilize their charges. Actually, the years prior to serious employment provide the only time when people can look over and reflect on the various fields without the bias acquired after they have committed themselves to one as a living. Most needed social changes are blocked by material and psychological investments that people make as they work in a certain field that not only provides a living but also submerses them in a subculture with its own frame of reference. Serious redirection of society will probably not occur if we don't enable some generation to investigate—during this stage of life when minds are least committed—both how we are making knowledge and how we are applying it.

Maybe we're partly ashamed for them to discover what we are doing until it's too late for them to do anything about it. But this is an era of declassification—for good reasons. We can't afford any longer to keep secrets that affect the welfare of all.

Kinds of Discourse

The other major common denominator of the specialized subjects is their expression in languages, ordinary and mathematical, which symbolize qualitatively and quantitatively whatever one is observing and reasoning about. So what makes a language different from empirical disciplines also makes it common to all.

Law schools, we're told, regard English majors as good candidates for admission, because in studying literature they have developed some sophistication about interpreting texts. Lawyers have to think of many possible interpretations of statutes and judicial decisions. Who else besides legal and literary professionals must do close textual analysis—look for ambiguity, spot implications, read for subtexts? Priests and preachers, interpreters of holy writ. Indeed, some scripture, like parts of the Old Testatment *is* law, and the long rabbinical traditions of arguing religious decrees on the basis of the Torah and the successive commentaries on it—the Talmud, and the Midrashim—may account for much of the affinity and ability Jews show for legal practice.

Literary critics, lawyers, and exegetes all practice the art and science of hermeneutics, of close textual analysis and of disputation citing not only some primal text like a poem, law, or scriptural passage but the texts of previous commentators. This art/science practiced across such different subjects requires bringing an extensive intertextuality to bear on intensive interpretation of a single text. For an example from one other profession, the analysts in diplomatic and intelligence offices also have to do exactly this when they interpret for their government the speeches, policy statements, and news releases issuing from foreign countries. Insofar as they have been cast into language and into text, different subject matters call for the same interpretive faculty regardless of the nature of the professions involved.

Discourse is a medium in which all subjects may be symbolized, however nonverbal may be their perceptual underpinnings. Putting knowledge into language tends to make all knowledge somewhat alike, because language imposes its forms and limits on it. This is true not only at the sentence level, where propositions are formulated, but at the level of a complete discourse.

A discourse is any kind of oral or written communication that is complete for its purpose—a dialogue or lecture, report or memorandum, poem or ad. Many kinds of discourse are common to all disciplines. Logs and journals, for example, may be kept about any topic by any observer who is in the middle of the events. Likewise, a news report, a psychiatric case history, an account of a physics experiment, an eyewitness deposition at a trial all run the gamut of subject matter but all share the narrative form of discourse, a story told after the conclusion of the events.

Essay imposes an organization different from either blow-by-blow journals or after-the-fact narratives. In an essay, statements follow an order of ideas, not an order of events. The dominant tense is not the progressive present ("the snow is falling") or the recent past of journals ("I have noticed lately") nor the past perfect of narrative ("she slammed down the phone and darted out") but the present tense of generalization ("doctors usually come from middle-class backgrounds"), which exists not to indicate time but to assert general propositions. Essays may contain stories but only to document statements. This form of discourse—generalization-supported-by-instances—may be employed to make statements about any subject whatsoever.

More abstract still is an argumentation, an essay not merely asserting and supporting a generalization but combining several generalizations so as to derive further generalizations. As narrative form mimics chronology ("then this and next this"), the essay of argumentation mimics the logical syllogism ("if this and this are true, then this must be true as well").

So in tracing the point that kinds of discourse keep their identities across different subject areas, that they in fact fit the subjects to themselves, we realize that by virtue of sharing these kinds of discourse, the various disciplines are related to one another and even become alike in some respects. This is so because kinds of discourse are really different vantage points from which a subject may be viewed or levels to which it may be abstracted. Kinds of discourse are ways of perceiving and thinking.

In fact, one revealing way to organize learning that cuts across subject areas is around kinds of discourse. I have for some time recommended this curricular change in the language arts so long as language should remain a separate subject in school. Students saturate themselves in one kind of discourse at a time, reading and writing and talking about a variety of subjects in the form of, say, dialogue or journal or report or short story or review or editorial.

Such reorganization would prove even more valuable for a totally integrated curriculum, especially when combined with another reorganization around interdisciplinary projects, as explained later. Allowing for differences in individual development, it's possible to sequence kinds of discourse so as to move from concrete to abstract and hence to exercise increasingly sophisticated mental faculties, as should become clearer in what follows below—the same faculties needed to carry out progressively more demanding interdisciplinary projects.

Levels of Abstracting

Take the forms of discourse mentioned above. Let's call the account told from within the events "recording" (the log or journal), the story told after the events "reporting" (the news story or case history), the thesis essay "generalizing," and the argumentative or syllogistic essay "theorizing." There are of course other sorts of discourse, and these four may often be found in mixture with these others as well as with one another, but the activities of recording, reporting, generalizing, and theorizing characterize the main spectrum of discourse and characterize it as successive ways of knowing something that carry a subject from observation through recollection to intellection—from sensation through memory to reason. For convenience, let's speak of these stages as successive abstractions and of these human faculties as various ways of abstracting experience.

What is common to the various subjects or disciplines is this abstracting or knowledge-making process, which the varieties of discourse reflect in a staged fashion correlating with the successive faculties and logics employed to make knowledge.

Recording and reporting are based on *chrono-logic,* time order, the "logic of the events." The essay of generalization is based on analogy or similarity among events or things, on the logic of classes, which we may call *ana-logic.* The essay of argumentation is based on the logic of propositions, on equations whereby saying this is tantamount to saying that as well, which we may call *tauto-logic.* We forge from the known to the unknown this way, by reasoning. The next step indeed is math, for verbal equations and syllogisms represent the threshold between the ordinary and the mathematical languages.

This progression also carries us from induction—distilling particulars into generalizations—to deduction—reasoning from one generalization to another. Inductive and deductive reasoning operate throughout all the empirical or worldly subjects we're considering here, which are based on thinking from sense-derived information. Surely, the investigative processes of observation, recollection, and intellection should undergird the general discursive curriculum, applying as they do from nonverbal perception into discourse and across the abstractive spectrum.

Kinds of Knowledge

But placing the subject-area disciplines along this spectrum of discourse also brings out what is unique about each and how they relate to each other. History, for example, is basically reporting, science basically generalizing, and philosophy basically theorizing. Mind you, these do overlap. When historians generalize about their narratives, they become social scientists. When scientists theorize from their generalizations they become philosophers. And when philosophers speculate about metaphysics, they become . . . mathematicians, as nearly all the great philosophers have been. Thus history, science, and philosophy differ by level of abstraction so as to form a continuum of knowledge-making bridging from particulars of the past to perspectives embracing all time.

This expansion across time and space is in fact a way to measure increasing abstraction. Each successive stage of it subsumes and builds on previous stages. In any subject, history leads to science, and science leads to philosophy, in just the way that records and reports provide the instances to generalize from and generalizations provide the propositions to syllogize with. Observation provides the material for recollection, and recollection provides the fodder for intellection. So, backwards, reason relies on memory and memory on sensation.

Going down the abstractive scale from history, we find the kinds of discourse of which history is made—biography and chronicle, which rest in turn on autobiography and memoir, which rest in turn on diaries and letters. “Source documents” become increasingly particular and personal, shrink to points in time and space, either the names and dates of archives and the entries in logs or the viewpoints of individuals ensconced in certain times and places.

Students reading and writing in these types of discourse are definitely studying history but also learning historiography, how history is made from successive distillations progressing from personal to public as it synopsizes more comprehensively across time and space. As narratives get more abstract they shift from first person to third person, from firsthand to secondhand and more remote sources. Working narrative at different ranges of the abstractive spectrum will teach students what kind of truth value to assign to the various stages of the cumulative cultural creation we call history.

Science is built on records and reports, but it abstracts particulars beyond *what happened* to *what happens*—a different order of fact and truth. The famous inductive or empirical approach of modern science consists, at least in principle, of observing first and reasoning later, of noting what happened on such and such occasion under natural or experimental conditions and of generalizing only after these field or laboratory notes have accumulated enough instances to generalize from. An anthropologist does not assume that a certain behavior is characteristic or ritualistic until she or he has seen it happen many times. These records are periodically reported in professional journals, say, as summary narratives followed by tentative generalization, an hypothesis to be borne out or not by subsequent observations by the same or other investigators. "Controlling the factors" means ruling out local contingencies that might account for what is observed and might thus defeat efforts to generalize across particular dates and places.

This disembedding of something from time and space partly defines the abstracting process. Thus many stories become one statement of fact. But as induction generates many such truths deduction comes into play to combine these so as to make them yield the hidden or implicit truths they collectively contain. These logical manipulations can occur at such a high level of abstraction that they can be carried out only in purely logical language devoid of all particularity, in mathematics. And so on with philosophy, the leaders of which have usually been mathematicians.

Organizing Around Projects

These ways of gaining and making knowledge are ultimately more important than particular contents, because a person well versed in inquiry processes can always become well informed about a certain subject, but someone who has only acquired information without learning how knowledge is made depends too much on memory and stock sources and does not understand, furthermore, how fallible and malleable knowledge is.

Besides, so much information exists today about so many subjects that decisions about which topics to present to students have become arbitrary. Which are "basic"? Which will be needed in the future? Then too, the concepts and information of the various fields change rapidly, and schools have always been the last to know, because specialized courses, textbooks, and teacher training change far more slowly, locking in the old and delaying the new far too long. Finally, decisions about which contents to offer, which to require, and which to leave as electives inevitably entail partisan preferences. Political, religious, ethnic, and commercial factions disagree about many of these decisions, which please some people only by displeasing others. In fact, the very incoherence and arbitrariness of traditional curriculum comes about in the first place from patching together concessions to such factions. Make no mistake about it, public education as we have known it is a political construction either favoring some classes and interests or frustrating all of them through compromise.

All this suggests a reorganization of curriculum away from teaching languages separately from contents and away from teaching contents in isolation from each other. Thus math and English would be practiced constantly through the content subjects, and the content subjects would be learned partly as factors of one another. But how to teach all the languages and contents through one another? Let's take our cue from the common denominator of the experiential subjects—knowledge-making itself, which combines such inquiry processes as observing and reasoning with the symbolization processes of the languages as they qualify and quantify the subject matter. Organize around projects that entail all these processes and that cut across subject areas. For these projects, students would investigate something, create something, or improve something. Instead of canning projects in advance, teachers would help students learn how to conceive and execute projects that embody their curiosity, aspiration, and practical intention.

This amounts to giving priority to the symbolizing rather than to the symbolized, to knowledge-making over some given knowledge. But of course students could not spend so much time learning how to learn without learning in the process a lot of information, more in fact than they acquire traditionally when information is programmed for them, because projects immerse the participants in some area of knowledge and entail further fact-finding.

A project can be short or long, done by a group or an individual. It does not focus on a field in the academic sense but rather, by embodying some desire to do or know something, usually cuts across fields and across divisions between verbal and nonverbal, mental and physical, or academic and vocational, as a project to counter some environmental pollution or health problem would naturally do.

Suppose, for an investigative example, some children are running an experimental project to find out which plant nourishment works best for certain plants in their windowbox garden. This entails keeping a log of the amounts and frequencies of watering and feeding with each food, setting up control samples for comparison, obtaining the plant foods, reading up on or asking around about the characteristics and needs of the plants, and disseminating project results partly through writing and the use of graphs and charts. Or a group wants to test various brands of batteries to see which are best and to do a consumer's report on batteries for other people to read. This could entail surveying consumers of batteries for their experiences and requirements, testing various batteries in various devices, reading what manufacturers say, reading up on the electrochemistry involved, taking apart and analyzing batteries of different brands, and so forth, in addition again to record-keeping, calculation, and dissemination of results in some medium. Such projects constantly call for new knowledge and skills in all areas, and students can be helped by older students and adults to find out what they need to know as they need to know it.

One project naturally leads to others, and all these concatenate into knowledge networks spreading well beyond the participants as others use or enjoy the creations or read or hear about what the participants found out. The rub-off effect from one working party to another is unbelievable until you have seen it. It alone would validate the principle of not teaching everybody the same things, of letting different working parties do different things at the same time.

Reorganizing curriculum around projects rather than around "subjects" would of course mean changing heaven and earth in schools. Students would be learning about all subjects via all symbol systems all the time. Fusing the curriculum can't possibly be separated from overall school reform because it calls for far more than just reconceiving what is to be taught. The very processes and organization of schooling itself have to be reconsidered and drastically altered. An entire set of conventional practices will have to be challenged—courses, classes, grade levels, textbooks, exams, and certification.

Scheduling biology or American literature once in a lifetime *looks* efficient in district curriculum guides because such courses present essentials in a systematic way, but in practice even students who receive A's in them forget most of what they learn because the very compactness and coherence by which the subject is presented makes permanently assimilating it very difficult. Where are the connections with other subjects, with real life, and with the individual learner's cumulative knowledge structures? Connections make all the difference. Making each subject self-contained and presenting it once, all at once, are very much to blame for the ineffectiveness of schooling. Good grades in the courses and good scores on the standardized tests merely mask this long-range ineffectuality.

But project-centered learning need not rule out some brief systematic presentations if these are elected by students at significant junctures in their knowledge-making. Such presentations need not be classes but could be a program of nature films, a videotaped lecture series, a set of activities on computer, laboratory practice, focused reading and discussion with a small group, or field experience working with professionals.

To combine the two main recommendations made above, subject matter could be reorganized at once around kinds of discourse and around interdisciplinary projects. This automatically grounds the curriculum in what subjects share—inquiry and discourse, that is, ways of investigating and ways of symbolizing. This also brings together subjects and languages, nonverbal and verbal learning.

In conceiving a project, the learners and helpers would consider how wide a range of the abstractive spectrum it might best span both to accomplish its practical objective and to teach the most. The two projects described above as examples could span a considerable range, since participants might be observing and recording, summarizing and reporting, generalizing and inferring as well as talking and reading at several levels of remove from physical objects. Much depends of course on the maturity and experience of the learners. But often the members of a working party carry out different parts of the project according to their wants and lights. And if the working party comprises people of different maturity levels, as it should, then every project could span an educationally useful range of thought and language. Less developed learners grow rapidly when collaborating on a project with more experienced colleagues.

The other main consideration in conceiving projects is experiential. The very idea of a project—to create, discover, or ameliorate something—keeps open all the possiblities of interaction with people and things—and of interaction between verbal and nonverbal. Methods of investigation derive in fact from basic sources of information, which are, precisely, people and things and previous people's investigation of things stored in the social environment. Projects keep languages and subjects in their right relationship of symbol systems to raw material.

Making, investigating, and ameliorating naturally overlap, whether the creation is a timing device for watering that windowbox garden over the weekend when no one is around or whether it's a book or performance. A project to create a multimedia performance is one way of researching personal or social experience and may at the same time be a way of initiating practical action such as helping children and seniors at risk. Because projects start with authentic motives to do and know, learners will either be simultaneously creating, investigating, and taking action in a single project or alternating these as one kind of project leads into the other. Art explores. It represents one mode of knowing that combines inquiry, human concern, and creation.

Rhythmic Curriculum

Mathematics requires special consideration in the curriculum. It is neither a factual subject nor is it a language learned spontaneously from infancy like English or Spanish or Russian. As the logical extension of any native language into higher realms of abstraction, it is the one truly universal discursive language. The farther the abstractive process removes things from physical reality, the more they come together. "Everything that rises must converge." This is as true of languages themselves as of the things they speak of. Just as mathematics subsumes the plurality of native languages into one purely logical language understood in all countries, so abstraction reduces the world from multiplicity to simplicity.

The remarkable thing, however, which needs examining now, concerns how the very abstractness of math as the quintessential logical language leads back again to concrete experience and the arts. *If seen in all its aspects,* math could act as a unifying field for a new curriculum, because it makes contact on all sides with other knowledge.

But to appreciate the point of this exception, we have to construe mathematics in a far broader way than is customary in the modern world, where it has been valued mostly for its practical applications and regarded as an adjunct of science. Seeing it only as a technical tool dehumanizes it and makes it harder to learn. But the very abstractness that seems to divorce math from basic human concerns was seen by the ancient world as a way of relating very different aspects of life to one another—music, for example, to astronomy, and both to the human body, the social body, and the body of this world they built on and navigated.

Math begins with counting and measuring physical reality and symbolizing these quantities in simple numbers. The calculations with these numbers that make up arithmetic are more removed but still relatively concrete. They allow us to manipulate counts and measurements of tangible things. Algebra abstracts arithmetic a step further; the same operations are used as in arithmetical calculation but operate upon letters, which stand for unknowns, that is, hypothetical quantities.

Math takes off from at least one other aspect of the material world than quantity alone—form. As its name says, geometry derived from measuring land. Being the study of shapes, it remains relatively close to materiality, although the shapes themselves, like numbers, do not designate physical objects but represent *classes* of objects. In adding a third dimension—volume to area—solid geometry increases the mental complexity but doesn't necessarily raise the abstraction level. Trigonometry is essentially just a practical means of using the constant relations of right-angle triangles to solve spatial problems—a specialized bit of geometry.

Except in rare advanced courses, unfortunately, these are the only sorts of mathematics usually attempted in public schools. (The movie *Stand and Deliver* told the true story of an inspiring exception.) Indeed, parents, teachers, and employers would be delirious if most students really learned these. Calculus, symbolic logic, and other sorts of higher mathematics that combine or build on one or more of these are usually reserved for college, where only math or science majors ever take them.

If math education were reorganized to bring out traits of it that connect well with familiar experience and with other sorts of knowledge, it would become easier to understand in itself and at the same time aid in understanding everything else. By taking advantage of math's many points of departure from physical reality and from ordinary language, and of the many connections among its own various forms, more of it could be learned in school, and better learned, than ever conceivable before.

Math's exceptional nature may justify some sorts of direct and continual presentation in schools that cannot be warranted for topical subjects and that is not necessary for the native language. But the nature of this new way of presenting needs to be deeply considered. Traditional courses will not do. Math in all its potentialities must pervade other learning and relate obviously to personal interests, for the rest of one's life.

Math and Literature

Accustomed as we are to thinking of reason and imagination as contrasting, or even opposing, we may have difficulty recognizing how kin math and literature may be. But consider that both reason and imagination reconstruct material reality in the mind and that both do so by abstracting it in some way. By the logic of classes, reason sorts the things of this world into mental bins, and then, by the logic of propositions, it states quantitative and qualitative truths about these classifications. Thought builds interlocking knowledge structures by combining these propositions in various logical ways to generate further propositions.

Imagination too disembeds and rearranges the objects of experience so as to form new constellations that in some way represent or symbolize the original reality. A novelist collages scraps of setting, incident, and character drawn from here and there, that is, "makes up" a story. But he or she reassembles reality for the purpose of charging it with meaning, just as the mathematician or scientist restates experience to reveal relationships not manifest before the particulars were disembedded. So both reason and imagination are creative and inventive. They differ only as alternative modes of knowing. After writing this section I became aware of Scott Buchanan's *Poetry and Mathematics* (1962), originally published in 1929, in which he argued that "each human being is both a poet and mathematician" by drawing parallels between aspects of literature and figures, numbers, proportions, equations, functions, and symbols.

Science employs public ways of classifying and syllogizing to build communal knowledge structures, whereas artists create idiosyncratic visions that are valuable because they supplement communal understanding with individual perception. But scientists contribute also out of personal intuition, and artists work with continuities passed on to them through the culture. And both are probably working off of archetypes common to everyone's mental life.

More specifically, math and literature have several affinities, ignored in the recent past, that a new curriculum should bring out. Both function through language, but both specialize language into a certain sort of discourse. Math moves language away from imagery and familiar objects toward logical purification, to the point of requiring special, abstract symbols. The language of literature continues to refer to familiar objects but makes of them "figures of speech," that is, refers *through* them to other things analogous to them. Thus fictional personages, events, settings, and objects become metaphors for counterparts existing in other times and places or on other planes of being. Plots are propositions, stories statements. Logic in literature is secreted—embedded and embodied in the character relations and the actions. While telling *what happened* (*once* upon a time) the fictioneer says *what happens* (*all* the time).

Both math and literature generalize reality, but the one does so through explicit abstraction that bares the thought process as nakedly as possible, the other implicitly by a kind of pseudoconcreteness that actually compresses several layers of reference into one set of referents. Metaphor does just this—refers simultaneously to two or more things that share some quality in common but that may lie in very different domains of experience. In literature, for example, twin siblings may symbolize any inner or outer thing that fluctuates between being one thing and being two, integer or fraction, or that may be seen sometimes as a whole, sometimes as separate, like two aspects of one person manifesting as independent behaviors.

Whereas math strives to eliminate ambiguity, literature exploits it for resonance. Math and literature both cast something in a new way so that it can be seen afresh. Math does this through explicit equation, literature through implicit comparison. Behind both is analogy. Both reassemble reality to know it better.

But literature relates to math not only discursively, as one specialized language to another, but also nondiscursively, as one art among the others. Literature differs from other uses of the native language not only in being more figurative but in being more rhythmic. What makes it artful are its nonverbal traits that it shares with music and dance, painting and sculpture—its proportions and periodicities, its rhythmic dynamism. Because ordinary language refers to things that can be seen, it evokes imagery. Because it can be vocalized, it can be rendered as sound. Because it is sequential, it moves in time. Sights and sounds, ideas and actions, can be played with like the stuff of any other art medium. What comes out in the sentences of literature as meter and cadence, rhyme and other sound play, comes out in the whole structure of a literary work as bigger forms of repetition and reversal, ratio and rhythm.

In fiction, drama, and poetry, the characters, events, settings, objects, or themes may all be orchestrated to create *patterns.* Characters may have foils or counterparts or exhibit telltale recurrent behavior. The personages and their actions may be counterpointed and harmonized to run the gamut of consonance and dissonance. Plots comprise all the dynamics, in fact, indicated in musical scores, such as accelerando and retardando, crescendo and decrescendo, largo and allegro, staccato and legato. Stories not only have themes but variations on a theme, which indeed is usually the very structure of a play or novel. All this is *patterning,* and both math and literature achieve what they do through it. The art of art is patterning, whatever its medium or material. By a marvelous arching out from ordinary discourse, math carries us beyond language and logic into what seems like a very different domain—the arts.

Math and Music

Music is the art of arts because it comes closest to pure self-referential structure and pattern. This basis in number—periodicity and proportion—constitutes its main affinity with math, which is also a mostly self-contained system. Because structure and pattern underlie both logic and art, they afford an invaluable bridge between activities generally thought to diverge as much as, stereotypically, accounting does from musical composing.

These aspects of math and music deserve special consideration inasmuch as this most transcendent art and this most abstract language both derive, paradoxically, from distinctly sensory experience. Tones are acoustical, and music is organized sound. Math begins, materially enough, with the counting, weighing, and measuring of things of this world, and through geometric shapes, graphs, and diagrams it combines visual with verbal. As its alliance with science and technology shows, it can be limitlessly applied to material and practical endeavors. It is both discursive and nondiscursive. Math and music are international semantics, one specializing in space, the other in time. They both concern the basic human sense of symmetry and asymmetry, consonance and dissonance, congruence and incongruence, equality and inequality. In quintessential form, these are expressed respectively as equations and ratios (balance and imbalance).

Like math, music deals with relationships. Even the tones of which it's made are just variant frequencies on a vibrational gradient. Their value or effect is relative to the other tones with which they are juxtaposed. A melody is just a series of shifts in pitch, of intervals, that are created by placing certain tones in a certain order. These pitch intervals are relationships among adjacent notes. So both tones and tunes are generated relationally.

The other main element of music is rhythm. In popular parlance, rhythm is a steady beat, but it is not merely that. It is two or more beats overlaying each other. Tap your foot at a certain constant rate. That's a beat. Now on every third tap pat one hand on some surface. Now you have rhythm, because regularly stressing a certain count creates a second beat overlaying the first. An overlay is a ratio between the frequency with which one beat falls and the frequency of the other. One stress every three counts is a waltz ratio. Melodies too generate beats that become part of the rhythm. The fact that some notes last several times as long as others sets up additional stress patterns. In other words, ratios of duration as well as of frequency may produce rhythm. Both concern timing—how often or how long something occurs in relation to when something else occurs. "In relation to" is the key.

But music has no exclusive claim to rhythm, which is a major constituent of all the other arts as well—not just the temporal or performing arts like dance but the spatial or graphic arts like painting. Things are measured or laid out against each other in either time or space—or space against time. When we speak of rhythm in the lines or color play of a painting, we do not even need to feel we're employing a musical metaphor. We know it means some kind of repetition or "echoing" of these lines and colors *in relation to* other elements in the painting. Rhythm is ratio—for so much of this, so much of that. By interrelating quantities it gives them qualities. It "puts things in proportion." Being entirely relational, in fact, rhythm transfers from one material domain to another, like number.

Both math and music are based on measure, ratio, and frequency. Actually, any measure is a ratio, because you can only measure something by placing it against something else, whether you're measuring time by a clock or space by a yardstick. For so much of this, so much of that. For every revolution of the earth around the sun we count 365 and a quarter rotations of the earth on its axis (days). For every half note, two quarter notes. For every quarter note, in 4/4 time, one beat. For every third beat, say, a stress. One thing is laid against another. Dividing thirty by six asks the ratio question, "For every thirty how many sixes are there?" ("How many sixes are there in thirty?") Percentages, fractions, and decimals are just different ways of expressing ratios: 30 percent means 30 for every 100, as do 30/100 and .30. Arithmetic is rhythmic and would be easy and pleasurable to learn if approached that way.

Math as a Humanity

The classical liberal arts quadrivium (of arithmetic, geometry, music, and astronomy) derived via Plato from the Pythagorean cosmology of musical/mathematical harmonics, which Pythagoras had transmitted from the East. Musicologist Ernest G. McClain has treated the Greek transmission of these cosmic harmonics in *The Pythagorean Plato: Prelude to the Song Itself* (1984), in which he argues that modern philosophers slight this key dimension to Plato's dialogues. In *The Myth of Invariance: The Origin of the Gods, Mathematics and Music from the Rig Veda to Plato* (1985), McClain demonstrates by means of tone-mandalas and tuning systems how central a role number and harmony played in antiquity's synthesis of knowledge, from India to Egypt. McClain took the "myth of invariance" from another original work on epistemolgy, *Hamlet's Mill: An Essay Investigating the Origins of Human Knowledge and Its Transmission Through Myth* (1977) by Giorgio de Santillana and Hertha von Dechend. They argue that under the countless myths of cultures all over the world can be discerned some constants—invariants—that, with the aid of numbers, the ancients had generalized about the world and had registered in myths, the story-statements through which they uttered their science. In the Preface, Santillana describes how this insight dawned on him.

> What is a solstice or an equinox? It stands for the capacity for coherence, deduction, imaginative invention, and reconstruction with which we could hardly credit our forefathers. And yet there it was. I *saw.*

> Mathematics was moving up on me from the depths of centuries; not after myth, but before it. Not armed with Greek rigor, but with the imagination of astrological power, with the understanding of astronomy. Number gave the key. Way back in time, before writing was even invented, it was *measures* and *counting* that provided the armature, the frame on which the rich context of real myth was to grow. (p. xi)

In *The Dimensions of Paradise* (1988), John Michell relates this astronomical measurement to terrestrial building. Preliterate cultures constructed their pyramids, temples, henges, and other stone- or earthworks not only according to seasonal astronomical alignments but also according to other "invariants" such as universal units of measure and certain ratios like pi and the golden mean that constituted a cross-cultural "sacred geometry." But to complete this curriculum of the ancients we have to return to music. To their applied sciences of planting, navigating, and building, which all depended on measuring time and space, we have to add the tuning of musical instruments, which required establishing tone scales based on ratios between acoustical frequencies.

A fusion of math and music unified this curriculum within the cosmology referred to in Part 2—the spectrum of rarer to denser planes of reality. These successive emanations, each "begot" from the one before, were mythified sometimes procreatively in the form of a *genealogy* of "gods" as transmitted through Homer and Hesiod or of more abstract spirits like Pronoia, Ennoia, and Sophia as transmitted through the Gnostics. Actually, when the names of these deities are directly translated—Chronos into Time or Pronoia into Foreknowing—we see the generic nature of what they personify. Given the supernatural capacities attributed to figures like Moses, the Biblical genealogies of ancestors served, like those of the deities, to symbolize a sort of Jacob's ladder between higher and lower planes.

As transmitted by Pythagoras and Plato, on the other hand, these successive emanations were expressed musically as overtones and undertones of each other and mathematically as multiples of each other. In combining math and music, this more abstract mode of expression not only avoided the pitfalls of literalism inherent in stories and personifications but did better justice to the cosmology. That is, the emanations are not really "successions" in time but octaves of reality generating each other only in the sense that one octave is a whole-number multiple of another—440, 880, or 1760 cycles per second, for example. Thus the multiple realities exist simultaneously and everywhere, intervibrating, so that everything and everybody is comprised of all octaves all the time.

In *Stalking the Wild Pendulum* (1977), engineer Itzak Bentov speculates brilliantly that successive emanations or octaves of reality could be created by means of what scientists today call "beat frequencies." That is, when a higher and a lower frequency intersect, their interference pattern creates a new frequency lower than either of the "parents." Thus any two adjacent frequencies could emanate a third, which could continue so propagating with still another until the subtlest reality were manifested in this way at the grossest level. Bentov proceeds to translate esoteric harmonics into modern harmonics, both represented by the oscillation of pendulums.

At any rate, it was that fusion of math and music that integrated the preliterate curriculum of antiquity. The world is very different now, and yet scientists speculating recently on the nature of the universe have begun to restore to math its earlier metaphysical function as the ultimate connector. If specialists in math, science, and music were willing to work with educators to explore the technical aspects of their disciplines within a framework of harmonics, once again construing math multidimensionally and humanistically, I feel that it would provide many leads toward creating a unified learning field.

Making math a humanity again comes down partly to restoring the overtones and undertones of number and measure. For the ancients, for example, numbers had qualities as well as quantities. Number one was wholeness, integrity, self-sufficiency, self-creation, divinity. Two was dichotomy, division, sexuality, and birth. Three was balance, unity across duality, mediation, and justice. As number one represented a point, two a line, and three a plane, four stood for volume, solidity, stability, and a pragmatic four-square orientation. Five combined the qualities of the numbers it summed—duality with trinity and quaternity with a new unity. (These were only some of the meanings of these numbers.) And so on, always extrapolating through resonance the quantitative traits of numbers into comparable qualities.

Things of the same quantity have similar qualities, no matter how otherwise unrelated. Think of the dynamics of threeness, whether the three items are vectors in a force field, participants in a discussion, or parties to an eclipse. Tracing the essential quality of a number across different items or subjects can create a fascinating cluster of meanings. Seven seems to be a fundamental period, as in the musical scale, the colors in the visible spectrum, and the maximum number of electron shells around an atomic nucleus. Things turn over on the octave, which may be why seven dominates the *Book of Revelations.*

The Theology of Arithmetic, attributed to the Neoplatonist Iamblichus, develops at length in this way the resonance of each number up to ten, one at a time. In *Number and Time: Reflections Leading Toward a Unification of Depth Psychology and Physics* (1974), Marie-Louise von Franz parlays this approach into an astonishing synthesis of esoteric harmonics and numerology with atomic physics, math, myth, and psychology, among other fields of knowledge. If this book alone were translated into curriculum, we would have the education of the future insofar as the integration of disciplines is concerned. She certainly makes the esoteric metaphysic respectable in terms of modern thought and knowledge, but she goes farther than this in utilizing such a cosmic framework to explore all the interrelations of the physical and the psychic.

To acknowledge that numbers have qualities would open up math education in one direction it needs to go—toward recognizable human experience. So far schools have attempted to connect math to life by applying it to practical problems as in arithmetical, algebraic, and geometrical calculations. Youngsters must indeed learn these—far better in fact than they traditionally do. But children don't start learning something for adults' practical reasons; they need personal connections. They can learn the number relationships from such concrete experiences as working with different numbers of partners or building structures with varying numbers of sticks—if the *meanings* of numbers are made a learning issue. Quantifying will be better learned through association with qualities. The deeper nature of math that made it part of the humanities until the scientific-industrial age should be restored, on peril both of perpetuating the current mental block against math and of not utilizing its natural potential to unify learning.

Reason as Rhythm

Of course a central strategy of math is to relate two different forms or expressions as an equation, which is a special one-to-one ratio, another way of laying one thing against another. Putting things in a ratio or an equivalence to each other constitutes so much of reasoning that the words *reason* and *ratio* stem from the same root—*ratio, rationis.* "To figure out" catches the connection between number and logic. The root idea of "reckon," underlying its double meaning of "to calculate" and "to reason," is "to bring together." And the etymology of both "reason" and "rhythm" reveals their kinship in the concept of *measure.* To "size up" something is to draw a conclusion about it.

But isn't this placing of things beside each other just what we also do when we make comparisons? Looking for similarity and difference results in the creation of categories or metaphors, in analogy, the logic of classification. Similarly, if inferring and syllogizing are ways of juxtaposing things so as to bring out their implications, then we may also regard the logic of propositions, tautology, as derived from the measuring of one thing against another. Thinking is relating, and the protoype of relating is the laying of one beat over against another to create a rhythm. This is the basic connection between math and music, the two most purely relational mental activities. Reason is rhythm.

For the ancients, ratio was not merely the fraction you get when two things are unequal. If things were not identical or equal, reason put them in relation by placing one over against the other, by measuring them against each other in the broadest sense. Humans deal with the bewildering pluralism of nature by matching and sorting things according to some private or public criteria about similarity and difference in form or function. Different objects mentally fitting the same quantitative or qualitative category, like statements saying the same thing in different ways, are equal or at least equivalent. Ratios are relations among things that do not match, that are not unitary, as symbolized by their being linked as a fraction. Far from negative, ratios make sure that everything is related to everything else despite differences. Ratios are rhythms—so much of this per so much of that. Reason is the great relater that harmonizes things across their differences by putting them in some rhythm to each other. It is therefore apt for dealing with the pluralism of creation, for making sense of it. In this fundamental meaning, ratio is not merely numerical nor reason merely formal.

True, it is reason itself that fractionates the world in the first place by cutting it up into objects not existing in the original unity of nature. But it balances this differentiation by integration, analysis by synthesis. At the very moment of sorting and matching, the mind is already relating—rebuilding—by virtue of the very system of categories and knowledge structures by which the sorting is carried out. Perhaps all building is rebuilding an underlying unity that for utilitarian purposes people have to dismantle to deal with. This concurrent tearing down and rebuilding compares to the processes of catabolism and anabolism that together make up metabolism.

As Plato said that the soul of the world is built on basic ratios (corresponding to the intervals of the octave, the fifth, the fourth, and the whole tone), scientists today tell us that reality is best understood as variations in frequency. A frequency is a ratio laying time against space—for every second, so many vibrations. At a low enough frequency, energy becomes matter. When you get to the bottom of things, *things* aren't there any more. All is relational. So the rhythmic view holds well for matter as well as for thought. The ultimate definition of reason—as rhythm—may base itself on a resonance between mind and matter, on the infinite connectedness of nature that mind, as a part of nature, discovers as it rebuilds nature within. (Part 1 of *Number and Time* (1974) is titled "Number Is the Common Ordering Factor of Psyche and Matter.")

Curiously, then, the generic, structural nature of mathematical language not only makes it continuous with everyday language but also makes it akin to the nonverbal arts and in fact to the rhythms of life itself, from the pulsations of blood and breath to the whirring and wheeling of stars and atoms. Perhaps abstraction does not remove us so far from life as first appears—something students should be learning over and over through myriad examples of the patterning that characterizes both thought and art.

Thinking as Making

Discursive learning should not be elevated above or otherwise separated from the learning of arts, crafts, and vocational skills, all of which require and develop the human functions we call thinking. However much we may not understand about thought—and may never understand—we can readily observe that it develops in coordination with eye, hand, ear, and other physical faculties. It is as if thinking occurs not just in the brain but across neural networks connecting the brain to other parts of the nervous system, which generally operates in holistic fashion. Furthermore, artistic and practical endeavors give people motives to think and other authentic circumstances in which to practice using their minds. This realism would of course be a major reason for organizing curriculum around projects.

The very notion of thinking seems grounded on making something, on *growth,* by analogy with a seed running its course from latency to fruition. Thus we speak of the ramifications (branchage) of an idea (germ of an idea). Above all, logic makes the "implicit" "explicit," terms whose etymology also reveals a growth model of unfolding. Likewise, in formal logic we deduce propositions from premises via syllogisms, that is, by chains of "if . . . then." Entailment is the key. As with the coded molecules of DNA, nothing is in the conclusions that is not in the premises. From all this we get an impression that thinking is constructing—building knowledge chains and structures step by step—to eventually cast a minimal idea into other *forms* that bring out its heretofore hidden potentialities.

But it is clear that many mental constructions, including those regarded as most creative in both the arts and sciences, occur, so far as we are able to observe them, in a single stroke. In fact, we want to call these "strokes of genius" or "moments of revelation." More soberly, we contrast this instantaneous, spontaneous production with deliberate, chain thinking and cast them into a dichotomy of intuition versus intellection.

But maybe the two processes differ only in their speed and visibility. If the chain that makes what is implicit explicit is buried or shortcut, we know only the conclusion, the product at the moment of manifestation. In other words, this highly touted distinction between inspiration and reason may be just another form of ignorance. Beethoven's notebooks indicate much revision and gradual construction, whereas Mozart seems often to have composed straight off, but the products were of the same sort and quality. Whether the composition be verbal, musical, mathematical, or physical, developing a theme or motif—which is nothing less than parlaying something given into something novel—should probably be acknowledged as thinking, without regard for how rapidly or overtly the psychlogical process occurs.

Suppose then, especially in view of the inconclusiveness of research on thinking, we treat thinking, for learning purposes, as mental building. This would allow us to talk in the same breath, without prejudice, about construing a text and constructing a physical apparatus, since both require "making something out of" some givens. Comprehending and composing mean literally "taking together" and "placing together," which tells us that making sense of something is very close to making something. Thinking and making both consist of putting one thing against another. In *Man the Musician* (1973), volume 2 of *Sound and Symbol,* Victor Zuckerkandl argues, as part of his case for *homo musicus,* that mathematical and musical thinking are making, because they make their own materials, just, he says, as God's thoughts are His creations.

Again, the things themselves about which we think, resemble the thinking. That is, the material reality that math, say, seems to remove us from is actually endlessly and essentially rhythmic, like thought itself. Consider the cycles in individual behavior and in history that syncopate and counterpoint each other. Or the interplaying periodicities of heavenly bodies. At the subatomic level, all matter is vibrational, not particulate. All the phenomena of physics studied separately in school—sound, light, electricity, and the various kinds of human-made and natural radiation—fall along a single frequency spectrum. The most fundamental aspects of any material subject in society and nature are its rhythms.

Rhythm, like reason, is the great relator, the most common denominator, the ultimate medium of exchange. However different otherwise, languages and subjects share it, verbal and nonverbal exchange occurs through it, and art and life meet in it. If some universal force is to integrate learning, then we want a rhythmic curriculum.

Learning as Attunement

Let's shift focus from the rhythm of knowledge to the rhythm of the knower, who is vibrating like the rest of nature. Direct knowledge of things means knowledge unmediated by discourse or by culture in any other form. Its impact is not consecutive but simultaneous. The effect is saturation, as in the expression "to be imbued" with something.

We can get some idea of such knowing from children in the first two or three years of life, before language and other socialization have substantially structured their consciousness. Not having conceptualized much of the world yet, and not yet very proficient at verbalizing, they rely on attunement to know what's up.

Tuning into other people and the environment works better the less distinct we feel from them. Being "open" or "receptive" really depends on the absence of boundaries, which inevitably become partial barriers. The small child does not distinguish much between self and world and indeed, until an ego structure forms to negotiate with the world, will have little of the sense of selfhood that older people are familar with. Inseparable from this ego structure arises a knowledge structure about the world and oneself that is necessarily partial but also somewhat obstinate. Preschool children learn fast because there's little to block their exchanging with the material and social environments. They get to know things by identifying with them and attuning to them.

Sometimes we say that people pick up knowledge by osmosis. This is a good metaphor, because osmosis depends on highly permeable membranes that permit fluids to pass easily in and out. Adults can sometimes learn nearly as rapidly as tots when in states and circumstances resembling those of infancy. Nothing is more important for future education than to understand what these may be. Identifying with other people and with nature certainly is a chief condition. When boundaries dissolve and defenses lower, attunement begins. How does this occur?

Well, we all begin life by identifying with the world and can regain this condition to the extent we can suspend our ego and the culture it is bound up with. This may happen at moments of extreme excitement or of unusual quietude. At both times we slip boundaries and are "transported." Where? "Beside" ourselves. But these are extremes, as in infancy. How about in daily life? Any time we focus intensely on some thing or activity, we approach this state. Hot motivation requires that the ego be willing to suspend itself somewhat for the sake of fulfilling its own will. This is how very determined adults can learn fast. They will submit to a tyrannical guru, forget what they thought they knew, quit defending themselves, identify more broadly than usual, or do anything else it takes to reach an intensely desired goal. They open up and get out of themselves. They become as a child.

If education enables people to identify broadly, minimize defensive egoism, and yet find things they want to do for intense personal reasons, this aids people enormously to develop or regain attunement. For contrast, consider traditional schooling, where children stay on guard against both staff and classmates, rarely decide what they do, and actually learn to tune *out* in order to insulate the self from all the impertinent institutionalism. The same three *i*'s that best further other sorts of learning—individualization, interaction, and integration—will also create the ground conditions for attunement. Plenty of warm human relations, of diverse nonverbal experience, of opportunities to connect all around, and of practice in making decisions will set the stage for learning by attuning while serving all sorts of other purposes. But they set necessary, not sufficient conditions.

It's no good to romanticize infancy. Preschoolers learn fast, but they may learn some awful things that will haunt them the rest of their lives. Precisely because they are so open and undefensive, they get indiscriminately imprinted by whatever happens around them, often indelibly as well. They absorb stimuli deep in, with virtually no screening, and connect these with little benefit yet of a developed knowledge structure. They telepathize without knowing it, so that they can't tell their minds from those of people around them. They obey, and disobey, unspoken commands. They imitate others unconsciously and as if the behavior were their own. In their trancelike state they are undergoing the equivalent of hypnosis but without having consented and without even being aware there is such a thing.

To avoid these disadvantages, the learner needs control and consciousness, a measure of which comes with increasing maturity and the normal growth of selfhood. But beyond this, schooling can do an enormous amount to facilitate attunement that does not usually occur in our culture without special education. Once beyond infancy, much depends on the refinement of the person. Someone not sensitive to certain signals will of course be unaware of the information they are beaming. Radio and television signals are passing through our bodies all the time without our "reading" them, because we are not sensitized to their frequencies. But it is difficult to know just how much people can learn by attunement because the "normal" range seems considerably lower than what many individuals are capable of.

Besides receptivity, good attunement requires keen sensory and kinesthetic perception, fine discrimination of ideas and imagination, a subtilized sensibility, and a higher consciousness. Many things in our society work against these, from bad eating habits and crude entertainment to gross values and heavy vibes. A refined person in this sense is not an easily hurt hothouse plant but a fine-tuned human organism capable of sending and receiving across the maximum frequency spectrum. Furthermore, because they are highly aware, such people can tune in and out of things at will.

We attune to what deeply interests us, to people or surroundings we spend much time with, to animals or materials we work or play with, to activities we observe or participate in. Typically, individuals are acute about some things and obtuse about other things. Any of these could be good or bad. Public education should not choose what students attune to but should create maximum access to other people, things, and environments. Influenced by plentiful interaction with others, individuals have to choose. But this education has to include practices in concentration and control of attunement that may sensitize everybody to everything. Nothing could be more apt here than making and hearing music, singing and dancing, which should be a daily part of school life.

The nervous system has to be quickened and sharpened and the body in general purified. What people eat, and how much, directly affect their sensitivity and receptivity. Foods vary in how toxic they are, how much they clog the cells, how assimilable they are, how long they linger in the body, and how much they affect glands. Waste removal is critical in purification and relates to the other key physical factor—activity. Some activities just build muscles, some circulate air and blood, some flush out the body, and some stimulate or balance glands. Because they secrete and regulate, glands affect many functions, including the electrochemical tuning of the body that in turn influences sensory, emotional, and psychic attunement. Physical education of the future would address not only health and skill but the capacity of the organism as an instrument of knowing.

The physical state is part of the overall state on which the capacity for direct knowledge depends. It interacts with the state of mind and consciousness. All fluctuate, partly according to focus, which is the key to attunement. Attention and concentration play paramount roles in learning of all sorts, including discursive. There's no question about it, sustaining focus makes things happen that don't otherwise—from logical culminations and intuitive leaps to breakthroughs in musical or athletic ability. When we dwell on or dwell in something exclusively for some time, we lose ourselves and take on some of the nature of that object, activity, or setting. In mechanical harmonics, when one thing—a pendulum, say—starts to move in time with some rhythm already established nearby, that's called entrainment. The thing is carried along or away by the activity. Likewise we start to resonate with what we're engaged with. That is attunement. Through it we come to know the object of our focus.

To focus, one must beam on one thing and let the rest fall away. Highly motivated activities naturally involve just this, but today's urban environments distract and jangle attention. Schools can try to arrange settings for concentration and practice in focusing. The Montessori schools set aside time for individuals to become rapt in some task, and many teachers are showing their youngsters how to get quiet, relax their bodies, empty their minds, and concentrate inwardly on some chosen image or idea. Preschool children who spent fifteen to twenty percent of their time "staring," reported Burton White (1975), were rated later in school as the brightest, happiest, and most charming. This staring is a natural form of meditation that may be directed inward or outward. The famous Professor Louis Agassiz of Harvard made his biology students gaze fixedly at a fish, say, until they virtually developed X-ray vision and could eventually see many things they couldn't at first. Focus may be fixed on objects or ideas, or on nothing.

Regularly quieting both body and mind allows the ego to go off duty for a while and for a person to slow or suspend inner chatter and hence the customary self-concern and worldview. To become a good receiver, stop transmitting for a while. Long-range, this habit can carry over to the rest of one's routine. It fastens one's being so securely that going out of oneself is less threatening. At the same time, it reduces stimuli so one notices what was drowned out before, like a faint instrument when the rest of the orchestra suddenly cuts off. So it is that apparently withdrawing from the world brings us closer to it. The best education would teach how to shift and hold attention either inside or outside and eventually how to remerge with the world at will. In an essay in *Coming on Center*, "Writing, Inner Speech, and Meditation" (Moffett, 1988), I have written more about some of these processes of attunement.

Such means of achieving direct knowledge, or gnosis, have long been regarded as spiritual discipline. Through attunement, knower and known become like one. Spirituality is wholeness, the reintegrating of the pluralism of the world into the primal unity underlying its differences. To attune is to let go of some individual differences long enough to experience the outside as the inside—and the inside as the outside. It thus risks identity but only to the extent one is unsure of one's own integrity. Centering practices can build self-esteem by consolidating the sense of self in independence of environment. The same activities that help one "get it together" for oneself also help us experience other things and other people the way we experience ourselves. Learning to know directly, to attune, naturally develops spirituality also, without rites and sermons.

Two main views of knowledge have vied for predominance in education since antiquity. According to the empirical mode, knowledge derives from material experience ordered by reason, as typified by investigative inquiry. According to the gnostic mode, knowledge comes from making ourselves consonant with what we want to know, since we and the world are related as undertones and overtones. These two views derive from differing assumptions about the relation of human nature to nature at large. In this respect, epistemology becomes metaphysical.

Our highly individualized modern consciousness inclines toward the empirical because it feels cut off from nature and so assumes that nature has "secrets" that have to be "wrested" from it by pursuing even farther the course of objectification that originally separated mind from matter. This means piecing together reality bit by bit through experimentation and inductive/deductive reasoning. In the meditative view, people may learn by resonance, by going into themselves in order to tune into things outside. This way of knowing assumes an underlying unity across nature that includes correspondences between inner and outer, mind and matter. These permit attunements between human nature and the rest of nature. If everything is consubstantial, the All is knowable through direct and total revelation in the instantaneous way attributed to intuition or inspiration, whereas the experiential learning by sense and reason slowly reunifies the world through successive approximations.

But educators don't have to resolve this metaphysical issue. They can plan for both empirical and gnostic knowing. Whether we are building the world on our own authority or rebuilding the long lost One, we do not need at once to know. We know that knowledge comes sometimes slow and partial, sometimes swift and whole. If we plan for youngsters to figure out the world, and at the same time to attune themselves to it, we can hardly go wrong. If nature is vibrant, and reason resonant, both modes can interplay in a single harmonic learning field.

Curricular Bibliography

Building a history curriculum: Guidelines for teaching history in schools. Bradley Commission. Education Excellence Network: Washington, DC, 1988.

Charting a course: Social studies for the 21st century. National Commission on Social Studies in the Schools, Washington, DC, 1989.

Curriculum and evaluation standards for school mathematics. National Council of Teachers of Mathematics: Reston, VA, 1989.

The English coalition conference: Democracy through language. Richard Lloyd-Jones and Andrea A. Lunsford, eds. National Council of Teachers of English: Urbana, IL, 1989.

National arts education accord: A Statement on arts education to governors and state legislators. American Alliance for Theatre and Education. Music Educators National Conference, National Art Education Association: 1991.

New perspectives and new directions in foreign language education. Diane W. Birckbichler, ed. National Textbook Company in conjunction with the American Council on the Teaching of Foreign Languages: 1990.

Project 2061: Science for all Americans. American Association for the Advancement of Science: Washington, DC 1989.

References

Alcott, B. (Ed.). (1837). *Conversations with Children on the Gospels.* (Vols 1–2). New York: Arno Press.

Armstrong, T. (1985). *The radiant child.* Wheaton, IL, and London: Theosophical Publishing House.

Aron, M. (1975). The world of the brain. *Harper's Magazine* 251 December: 3–4.

Attar, Farid Ud-Din (1954). *The conference of the birds* (Nott, Trans.). New York: Samuel Weiser.

Becker, Robert O., and Selden, G. (1985). *The Body electric: Electromagnetism and the foundations of life.* New York: William Morrow.

Bennett says Stanford "capitulated." (1988). *San Francisco Chronicle,* April 19.

Bentov, I. (1977) *Stalking the wild pendulum.* New York: Bantam.

Bernal, M. (1987). *Black Athena: the Afroasiatic roots of classical civilization.* (Vols. 1–3). New Brunswick, NJ: Rutgers University Press.

Besant, A. (1896, 1960). *Man and his bodies.* Adyar, Madras, India: Theosophical Publishing House.

Bohm, D. (1980). *Wholeness and the implicate order.* London and Boston: Ark.

A book for burning? (24 September 1981 vol 293, no. 5830) *Nature* 293: 245–46.

Buchanan, Scott. (1962). *Poetry and mathematics.* New York: J. B. Lippincott.

Budge, E. A. W. (1895). *The Egyptian book of the dead.* New York: Dover.

Burke, K. (1961). *The rhetoric of religion: Studies in logology. Berkeley: University of California Press.*

Capra, F. (1977) *The tao of physics.* New York: Bantam.

Capt, E. R. (1979). *Our great seal: The symbol of our heritage and our destiny.* Thousand Oaks, CA: Artisan Sales.

The challenge of black Athena (1989). *Arethusa, special issue (Fall). Buffalo: Department of Classics, State University of New York.*

de Barruel, A. (1911). *Mémoires pour servir à l'histoire du jacobinisme. Paris: F. Le Prat.*

de Santillana, G., and von Dechend, H. (1977). *Hamlet's mill: An essay investigating the origins of human knowledge and its transmission through myth. Boston: David R. Godine.*

Dyson, A., and Freedman S. (1991). Writing. In J. Flood, J. Jensen, D. Lapp, and J. Squire, (Eds.), *Handbook of research on teaching the English language arts.* New York: Macmillan.

Eco, U. (1988). *Foucault's pendulum.* New York: Ballantine.

Faÿe, B. (1935). *Revolution and freemasonry, 1680–1800.* Boston: Little, Brown.

Farr R. (1981, 1986). *What research says to the reading teacher: Trends and challenges.* Washington: National Education Association.

Fromm, E. (1941). *Escape from freedom.* New York: Holt, Rinehart, & Winston.

Frye, N. (1976). *The secular scripture: A study of the structure of romance.* Cambridge, MA: Harvard University Press.

———. (1980). *Creation and recreation.* Toronto: University of Toronto Press.

———. (1981). *The great code: The bible and literature.* New York: Harcourt Brace Jovanovich.

Furth, H. (1966). *Thinking without language: Psychological implications of deafness.* New York: Free Press.

Gardner, H. (1987). *Balancing specialized and comprehensive knowledge: the growing educational challenge,* an oral presentation at the Southwestern Bell-Breckenridge Forum Conference in San Antonio, Texas, August.

Hall, M. P. (1978). *The secret teachings of all ages: An encyclopedie outline of Masonic, Hermetic, Cabalistic, and Rosicrucian Symbolical Philosophy.* Los Angeles, CA: The Philosophical Research Society Inc.

Havelock, E. A. (1986). *The muse learns to write: Reflections on orality and literacy from antiquity to the present.* New Haven, CT: Yale University Press.

Heckethorn, C. W. (1965). *The secret societies of all ages and countries.* New Hyde Park, NY: University Press.

Heindel, M. (1909). *The Rosicrucian cosmo-conception.* Oceanside, CA: The Rosicrucian Fellowship.

Huxley, A. (1944). *The perennial philosophy.* New York: World.

James, M. R. (1924). *The apocryphal new testament.* Oxford, England: Clarendon Press.

Jaynes, J. (1976). *The origins of consciousness in the breakdown of the bicameral mind.* Boston: Houghton Mifflin.

Koestler, A. (1972). *The roots of consciousness: An excursion into parapsychology.* New York: Vintage

Legge, J. (Tr.). (1882). *I. ching: Book of Changes.* New York: Causeway.

Michell, J. (1985). *The new view over Atlantis.* New York: Harcourt Brace Jovanovich.

———. (1988). *The dimensions of paradise: The proportions and symbolic numbers of ancient cosmology.* London: Thames & Hudson.

McClain, E. G. (1985). *The myth of invariance: The origin of the gods, mathematics, and music from the Rig Veda to Plato.* New York: Nicolas-Hayes.

———. (1984). *The pythagorean Plato: Prelude to the song itself.* New York: Nicolas-Hayes.

Miller, K. (1985). *Doubles: Studies in literary history.* New York: Oxford University Press.

Moffett, J. (1988). *Storm in the mountains.* Carbondale: Southern Illinois University Press

———. (1988). Writing, inner speech, and mediation. In *Coming on center: Essays in English education.* Portsmouth, NH: Boynton/Cook-Heinemann.

Neff, G. T. (1990). *Writer's market.* Cincinnati, OH: Writer's Digest Books.

Penfield, W. (1975). *The mystery of the mind: A critical study of consciousness and the human brain.* Princeton, NJ: Princeton University Press.

Pearce, J. C. (1977). *The magical child.* New York: E. P. Dutton.

Plato. (1929). *Timaeus.* (Vol. 7 of Plato in the Loeb Classical Library). Cambridge, Ma: Harvard University Press.

Powell, A. E. (1969). *The etheric double: The health aura of man.* Wheaton, IL: Theosophical Publishing House.

Pribram, K. H. (1982). What the fuss is all about. In K. Wilber (Ed.), *The holographic paradigm and other paradoxes.* Cambridge, MA: Shambhala.

Resnick, L. (1987). *Education and learning to think.* Washington: National Academy Press.

Roberts, J. M. (1972. *The mythology of the secret societies.* New York: Scribner.

Robinson, F. N. (Ed.) (1933). *The poetical Works of Chaucer.* Boston: Houghton Mifflin.

Rosenshine, B., and Stevens, R. (1984). Classroom instruction in reading. In P. D. Pearson, (Ed.), *Handbook of reading research.* New York: Longman.

Sagan, C. (1977). *The dragons of eden.* New York: Random House.

Scott, W. (1924). *Hermetica: The ancient Greek and Latin writings which contain religious or philosophical teachings ascribed to Hermes Trismegistus.* (Vols. 1–4). London: Dawsons of Pall Mall.

Shah, I. (1964). *The Sufis.* Garden City, NY: Doubleday Anchor.

Sheldrake, R. (1981). *A new science of life: The hypothesis of formative causation.* Los Angeles: J. P. Tarcher.

Sheldrake, R., and Bohm, D. (1982). Sheldrake, Bohm, and morphogenetic fields and the implicate order. *Revision: A journal of Consciousness and Change.* Vol 5, no 2. Fall 1982 (pp 41–48).

Solotaroff, T. (1991). The paperbacking of publishing. *The nation* October 7, 1991: vol 253, no 11: 399–404.

Steiner, R. L. (1957). *Occult history.* London: Rudolf Steiner Press.

Taylor, M. C. (1984). *Erring: A postmodern a / theology.* Chicago and London: University of Chicago Press.

Venezky, R. (1984). The history of reading research. In P. D. Pearson (Ed.), *Handbook of reading research.* New York: Longman.

von Franz, M-L. (1974). *Number and time: Reflections leading toward a unification of depth psychology and physics.* Evanston, IL: Northwestern University Press.

Watersfield, R. (Tr.) (1988). *The theology of arithmetic.* Grand Rapids, MI: Phanes Press.

Watson, L. (1979). *Lifetide: The biology of the unconscious.* New York: Simon & Schuster.

Webster, N. (1924). *Secret societies and subversive movements.* Christian Book Club of America.

White, B. (1975). *The first three years of life.* Englewood Cliffs, NJ: Prentice Hall.

Westman, R. S., and McGuire, J. E. (1977). *Hermeticism and the scientific revolution.* Los Angeles: William Andrews Clark Memorial Library, University of California.

Yates, F. (1979). *The occult philosophy in the Elizabethan age.* London: Ark.

Zuckerkandl, V. (1956). *Man the musician.* (*Sound and Symbol: Music and the External World* Willard Trask (Tr.). New York: Pantheon. Princeton, NJ: Princeton University Press.